PRAISE FOR
MANAGER'S DESKTOP CONSULTANT

"An invaluable new resource for leaders and managers, with live examples and compelling philosophy that will help them learn, grow, and become more effective, compelling, and fulfilled. It's a leadership handbook for the future."
—**Frances Hesselbein, Chairman and Founding President,**
   Leader to Leader Institute (formerly the Drucker Foundation
   for Nonprofit Management)

"Truly an 'hour consultant on the shelf.' Essex and Kusy offer great prescriptive solutions through their balanced advice. Their point-counterpoint approach helps to look at the multiple sides of dealing with classic organizational problems. All of our young executives need to be exposed to this wealth of professional advice. Having just gone through a major organizational integration, I know these are proven solutions on dealing with the human issues."
—**Frank Guzzetta, Chairman and CEO, Macy's North**

"A delightful addition to a very small library of books that can actually help the manager who needs some quick and intelligent advice. I have no doubt that you will find many who thank Essex and Kusy for the decision trees as a quick way to size up a situation. Managers beg for this stuff."
—**Stephen C. Lundin, PhD, FAIM, author of**
   Fish!, Fish Sticks,* and *Top Performer

MANAGER'S DESKTOP CONSULTANT

LOUELLEN N. ESSEX
MITCHELL E. KUSY

Manager's Desktop Consultant

JUST-IN-TIME SOLUTIONS
TO THE TOP PEOPLE PROBLEMS
THAT KEEP YOU UP AT NIGHT

Davies-Black Publishing
Mountain View, California

Published by Davies-Black Publishing, a division of CPP, Inc., 1055 Joaquin Road, 2nd Floor, Mountain View, CA 94043; 800-624-1765.

Special discounts on bulk quantities of Davies-Black books are available to corporations, professional associations, and other organizations. For details, contact the Director of Marketing and Sales at Davies-Black Publishing: 650-691-9123; fax 650-623-9271.

Davies-Black and its colophon are registered trademarks of CPP, Inc. Myers-Briggs Type Indicator is a trademark or registered trademark of the Myers-Briggs Type Indicator Trust in the United States and other countries.

Visit the Davies-Black Publishing Web site at www.daviesblack.com.

Printed in the United States of America.
11 10 09 08 07 10 9 8 7 6 5 4 3 2 1

Library of Congress Cataloging-in-Publication Data
Essex, Louellen.
    Manager's desktop consultant : just-in-time solutions to the top people problems that keep you up at night / Louellen N. Essex and Mitchell E. Kusy.
    —1st ed.
      p. cm.
    Includes bibliographical references and index.
    ISBN 978-0-89106-233-2 (pbk.)
    1. Communication in management. 2. Management. I. Kusy, Mitchell.
    II. Title.
    HD30.3.E77 2007
    658.4′092—dc22
                                                                          2007016037
FIRST EDITION
First printing 2007

*To our mothers, who have
guided us along the way
through their continuous
support and love*

Contents

About the Authors

Louellen Essex

Louellen Essex, PhD, is an organization learning and development consultant specializing in leadership, communication, team building, and conflict resolution. She is a Fellow of the Carlson School of Management's Executive Education Center at the University of Minnesota and an adjunct faculty member at the University of St. Thomas in Minneapolis, Minnesota. She has received the Professional Excellence Award from the American Society for Training and Development for her work in management development.

Essex has worked extensively with Fortune 500 companies, health care organizations, government agencies, and nonprofit organizations. With Mitchell Kusy, she coauthored *Fast Forward Leadership* (Financial Times Prentice Hall, 1999), which describes how to exchange outmoded practices for forward-looking leadership, and *Breaking the Code of Silence: Prominent Leaders Reveal How They Rebounded from Seven Critical Mistakes* (Taylor Trade, 2005).

Mitchell Kusy

Mitchell Kusy, PhD, has twenty-five years of experience in leadership and organization development. A registered organization development consultant, he is a full professor in the PhD program in leadership and change at Antioch University, Ohio, and a distinguished visiting professor at the University of Auckland, New Zealand. He recently received the honor of being selected a Fulbright Scholar for international organization development and, in 1998, was named Minnesota Organization Development Practitioner of the Year.

Before entering academia, Kusy worked in industry and directed the leadership development area at American Express Financial Advisors; previously, he managed organization development for Health Partners. He consults internationally in leadership development, strategic planning, team development, 360-degree feedback, executive coaching, and organization development.

Why Manager's Desktop Consultant?

If you are like most of the managers we know, you're busier than ever before, constrained by limited time and resources. Your organization has streamlined its structure and reduced the number of staff. You are finding that your task list gets longer every day. Problems crop up—especially "people" issues—that require your attention, and the solutions are not immediately apparent. You need help! Even when assistance is available from human resource specialists or internal consultants, these staff members are often backlogged, making just-in-time assistance a true challenge to obtain. Funds for hiring an outside consultant often are not available. And sometimes you might be reluctant even to seek help in the first place, worrying that you could appear inadequate, so you opt to go it alone. *Manager's Desktop Consultant* is our way of helping you meet the challenges you face.

In this book, we help you maneuver through the myriad of issues and challenges you encounter as a leader in your organization. In essence, we'll become your guides, offering the next best thing to a personal leadership coach or a management consultant. We'll save you time and money by helping you solve organizational problems without a consultant. But should you determine that you need some consulting help, this book gives you a quick way to get background on the issues you are facing so that you will be better prepared to work with a consultant in person.

In an effort to design the most meaningful and practical book, we analyzed hundreds of situations in which we have intervened as consultants. We pooled our experiences to give you answers to the most typical problems our clients have brought to us. By sharing the advice we have given, we hope to work side by side with you, coaching you to find optimal solutions to your challenges with relative ease. Our methodology can be easily placed into two basic approaches. First, we analyzed the problems our clients brought us and collapsed these into six areas representing the most critical issues they face: managing and leading change, building collaboration and teamwork, managing performance issues, managing conflict, dealing with organizational politics, and establishing oneself as a new leader. Second, we reviewed the types of solutions we proposed to clients for each of these areas and created a general menu of actions for leaders to consider.

While we view executives and practicing middle and upper managers as the primary audience for this book, we anticipate that it will be useful to management consultants as well. We hope that when these two target audiences interact, our book will enhance their agility in communicating with each other. With the more comprehensive view of both perspectives that results, greater buy-in and success are likely to occur.

For each of the six areas, we offer a quick overview of what we believe to be the most useful information related to the specific topic. We have gleaned the best tips from other books and then added our own views based on our consulting experiences. Next, in order to help you choose a strategy to tackle your management problem, we present a decision-making flowchart and provide scenarios designed to show you how to apply the information in real life. Both of us give our advice on how the scenarios might be effectively addressed. You'll see that, at times, our advice is similar. In other instances, however, we give differing advice—demonstrating the range of options available. We are confident that the scenarios we've developed are quite similar to situations you are facing.

As you finish reading each chapter, you should be more comfortable in dealing with these issues on your own and become more adept at using consultants to help you should the opportunity arise. Ultimately, we believe that our readers will be much more able to choose the best approach for a given situation and have a successful outcome, whether they are leaders or management consultants.

Each chapter in this book focuses on one of the six most critical needs of managers when it comes to dealing with human interactions. Here's a brief rundown.

In Chapter 1, we address the challenge of managing and leading change. In our work with thousands of managers worldwide over the past twenty-five years, we have found that leading change is often the issue on which they seek our advice. Change is occurring at unprecedented rates, and all managers, from novices to senior-level executives, must know how to lead it.

We tackle three leadership situations in managing change. The first concerns working with staff who resist change. In this situation, managers must contend with a tremendous drive to maintain the status quo—the staunchest inhibitor of successful and positive change. Why? Because to some, the unknown is far worse than the current situation, even if what's going on now isn't that great! The second situation involves developing a change management plan that will work. We find it interesting that even some of the most structured managers take an ad hoc approach to change management. So we address the critical components of building a viable action plan with engagement from key stakeholders. We also focus on how to structure a plan with insight, engagement, and realism. The third situation relates to creating a strategic planning process. Some managers relegate strategic planning to the executive domain and therefore believe it is beyond the scope of their expertise or control. As you'll see in this chapter, our intent is for all leaders to have the skills to engage more effectively in strategy formulation. We have also observed the consequences of the manager who designs the plan solo and then seeks buy-in from others. This approach is usually ineffective because people typically want involvement during the early stages of the process. Chapter 1 provides guidelines for engagement right from the start. This creates better results and ownership of all involved.

After reading Chapter 1, you should be on your way to taking the helm and going through the steps of designing a strategic planning process that adds true value to the organization. Note that we said you would design the "process," not the "plan." In our experience, a plan is almost worthless if it has not pulled in critical input from others. In Chapter 2, we focus on the key components of building collaboration and teamwork. We hold the perspective that team building is not just "nice to do" or a touchy-feely exercise in hand-holding but rather an essential part of creating productivity and efficiency.

The first section of Chapter 2 introduces the concept of building collaboration within an intact work-unit team. The second and third sections address collaboration within a work unit and within a cross-functional work team comprising members from different work units, and teamwork across multiple work units—that is, interteam development. There certainly are some similarities among these types of team building, but there are also significant differences that must be taken into account. In this chapter, we assist leaders in exploring these contrasts with practical and concrete outcomes. The fourth section provides guidance on facilitating a team-building retreat. Although some of these sessions are best conducted by an external consultant, the manager may take responsibility for this activity in specific contexts. We also include advice on facilitating an annual retreat and making the event meaningful, so that it results in specific actionable items that will make the team stronger.

Chapter 3 identifies the major dilemmas associated with managing staff performance. In the hundreds of 360-degree feedback processes we have facilitated over the years, this is one area in which both managers and staff note huge problems. Managers often say that this is one of their biggest challenges and lament their perceived ineffectiveness. Likewise, we have found that staff often want more direct feedback on their performance.

In the first section of this chapter, we discuss the challenges inherent in assessing staff performance problems. Then we offer strategies for working with staff members who don't carry their weight—the number one issue in work group dynamics. We then address the concerns of employees who fall below standards. These issues are related but subtly different and therefore require individualized practical action strategies. The third section of the chapter centers on staff members who are ineffective in working with others. They may certainly be successful individual contributors, but in the world of talent management, no person is an island. The twenty-first-century organization is calling for the skills of many incorporated into a final product or service. Here, we provide support for leaders who need to engage their talent in a collaborative way via effective management of team members' performance. Finally, we delve into an area that has gone largely unnoticed by many leaders—managing organizational "stars." Quite frankly, managers often don't think about providing consistent attention to their high performers. Sometimes they even ignore them (not intentionally but, rather, because they are "low maintenance"). This deleterious situation can lead to extremely negative consequences for leaders, stars, and their organizations. We help managers see how managing the performance of their organizational stars is significantly different from managing problem performers. In addition, we provide templates that explain what leaders need to do for both their stars and their poor performers.

Conflict management, the topic of Chapter 4, is closely aligned with performance management. At times, the two go hand in hand, and we suggest that managers read Chapters 3 and 4 in tandem. Leaders need to discern the best practices for working effectively with peers who simply aren't team players. In Chapter 4, we begin with a tool to help you determine how well you have prepared the work environment to deal with conflict—the Organizational Conflict Predictor. Then we discuss five specific conflict management approaches and provide a revealing questionnaire to help you assess your preferred approach. We go from there to discuss the art of communicating in conflict situations. Finally, we address some options for managing specific conflict-ridden dynamics: dealing with peers who aren't team players, establishing a working relationship with a difficult boss, and working with a peer who is problematic.

Chapter 5 addresses the power of building a base of influence through the understanding of organizational politics. In our view, *politics* is not a dirty word, and competent engagement in the dynamic is essential to leadership success. First, we discuss the importance of gaining understanding about how things get done in the organization. Then we describe how to influence others more effectively, creating a base of influence and utilizing power as a means of driving initiatives that result in goal attainment. Next, we concentrate on how leaders garner credibility and recognition for themselves and their staffs. Some leaders are self-effacing and don't want the attention—a big mistake. We redirect this focus by explaining the critical importance of this PR role in gaining success.

If you're a new leader, you'll want to pay particular attention to Chapter 6, which addresses how to position yourself in your recently acquired role. We discuss strategies for entering a new group and making a successful transition to the role of leader. We offer some of the tips we have found successful over the years—what leaders have done as well as what we as consultants have facilitated with our own clients. As new managers begin to establish themselves, problems may arise. For many, the question of how to work with staff who do not support their endeavors is at the top of the list, and we offer guidance on how to approach this delicate situation.

Finally, in the epilogue, we offer some guiding thoughts that synthesize the underlying philosophy of our views on management and leadership.

We hope you see the value in the unique approach of *Manager's Desktop Consultant*. We believe that no other book offers advice based on real-life situations drawn from the authors' consulting practices and presents two viewpoints for each problem. You'll see that we discuss the situations as if the characters in the scenarios were asking us directly for advice. The flowcharts in each chapter give the leader or consultant a way of succinctly and strategically analyzing the cause of a given problem and the path to the best solution, thereby teaching a problem-solving approach.

We have had a great time writing this book. As consultants, we felt a particular energy around collapsing much of what we do into a few hundred pages. This was no easy task! It forced us to merge the complex processes we often had in our minds and turn them into something concrete. We hope you will become a better leader as a result of integrating some of the advice we offer in *Manager's Desktop Consultant*. Our best to you!

CHAPTER 1

Managing and Leading Change

IN OUR CONSULTING PRACTICES, we have found that many managers lack the skills necessary to operate effectively in their often precarious change management roles. With pressures from above, below, and beside them within the organizational structure, many who lack a well-established set of guidelines for change management become confused. In this chapter, we deal with three specific scenarios, sharing the advice we often give our clients as they work through the muddle of managing and leading change. First, we address dealing with staff resistance, the most common problem managers bring to us. Second, we discuss creating a change management plan, a step that is often performed ineffectively, if at all. Third, we give advice on when and how to design a strategic planning process focusing on change, in the future tense.

Avoiding overreaction is the critical theme in all three sections of this chapter. You will see that, with a series of well-planned and well-orchestrated drives, managers can significantly increase the probability of successfully launching change with the least amount of overreaction and, ultimately, the least resistance.

Managers who intend to be successful in guiding change are faced with a twofold challenge. Sometimes, they are charged by senior leaders to implement a change that is not of their choosing, which they may or may not support. Serving as intermediaries, middle managers must translate the communication about the need for change and the accompanying plan of action to staff members in a manner that motivates them to move forward. At other times, managers are the change initiators, embarking on a new direction of their own or their staffs' design. In this case, they must acquire the organizational resources and support needed to drive action.

Managers must have a complex set of skills in the change management arena. They must know how to communicate persuasively and have a keen understanding of their audience and of how best to position their argument. Given that not all staff members will readily accept change, managers must develop the ability to empathize, listen, and problem-solve when they meet with resistance. When taking the lead in change, managers need to plan skillfully by setting measurable goals and creating strategies for obtaining them. Throughout the change process, managers must motivate those involved to remain diligent in implementing a new way of doing things.

DEALING WITH STAFF RESISTANCE

Decision analysis is key in developing an approach to any kind of staff resistance. Why is this so important as an initial step? Our answer has two components. First, it serves as a stopgap measure, forcing the manager to take time to think through what's going on. With this extra time, the manager is less likely to overreact. Second, decision analysis provides the manager with an opportunity to design a better process for dealing with staff resistance to change. In this mode, the manager has a system in place for responding to staff resistance. After all, would a good manager make a decision regarding a critical area of concern without adequate analysis? We hope not. Likewise, why would a successful manager determine how to deal with staff resistance without significant reflection and assessment? The flowchart in Figure 1 illustrates our perspectives.

FIGURE 1. **Flowchart for Dealing with Staff Resistance**

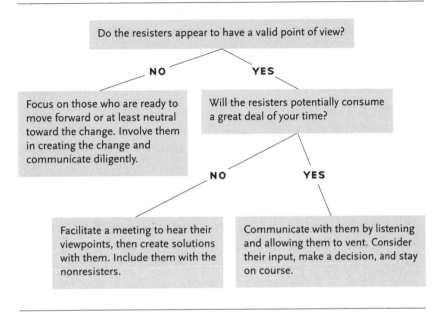

CONSIDER RESISTERS' CLAIMS

Let's carefully consider this flowchart and try to understand why these questions are so important. One of the biggest mistakes we have seen managers make at this stage is to work too much with resisters who have illegitimate claims—invalid points of view, if you will. Therefore, we suggest that the very first question the manager consider is whether the resisters' claims are valid. If not, extensive research evidence suggests that the leader should spend less time with the resisters and more time working with those who are gung-ho for the change or are at least neutral about it. Why? Think about it this way. Who often has the most influence over a person's action—someone in authority or one's peer group? Yes, we know that an authority figure can certainly dictate how things are going to be done. But is this the best person to advocate for long-lasting change? We suggest you pause and truly think about your response to this question. Think about your kids, spouse, friend, significant other, a colleague, or anyone in your social or professional network. Enduring change results in large part from the efforts of those who have influence over us. Likewise, think about what motivates you. If we were to ask what would produce a positive change in your performance, some of you might respond by saying "money." Yes, money is certainly a motivator, but not a long-term one. In many ways, we liken authority figures to money. They can certainly produce change in behaviors but, we believe, not long-lasting ones. Consider this scenario. If your boss were to give you a $10,000 increase in salary, we believe your performance would improve, albeit temporarily. Once you became used to this new salary, however, your performance would probably plateau or maybe even go back to its original level.

The issue here is the validity of the resistance. Sometimes it is a signal that the change is ill-conceived and should be reconsidered or that some aspect of the change process is flawed. The manager needs to think about who is resisting. If the resistance is coming from highly committed and credible staff members, then what they have to say may be quite valid. If, however, the source of resistance is staff members with poor performance records and a history of complaining with no evidence to back up their claims, then the manager may want to continue on course. In either case, it is important to listen before judging.

FOCUS ON THOSE WHO MOVE FORWARD

So now, back to our original proposition. If the resisters do not have a valid point of view, focus your efforts on those who are pro-change. In general, management literature gives strong evidence that with any change effort, 20 percent of the group will quickly accept the change, 70 percent will get on board if the leader follows a reasonable process, and only 10 percent will be hard-core resisters. Make certain you do not neglect those who are proponents of change and then really use them to promote the change effort. This goes back to what we just said about influencers of change. Use these pro-change individuals first to influence the nonresisters and help get them on board. If this fails, we suggest that you allow some good performance management systems to kick in. So much has been written on how best to manage performance that we don't believe it's necessary to repeat the models here. However, in general, we recommend that you at least set expectations and make sure the resisters understand these expectations, monitor their performance closely and consistently, provide feedback in behavioral terms, and then hold them accountable with actionable consequences if they don't deliver on the expected changes. For a more detailed breakdown of the performance management process, you may want to jump ahead to Chapter 3, "Managing Performance Issues."

As much as possible, involve the 90 percent (the 20 percent plus 70 percent identified in the previous paragraph) who are at least somewhat receptive to the change. In one study after another, it has been estimated that approximately 50 percent of all organizational change projects fail. The reason? Lack of buy-in right from the very beginning. It's the "people stuff" that really makes a difference. And not just with small projects. It applies to huge projects, such as mergers, which exhibit even more phenomenal statistics. Across the board, a myriad of reputable studies offer strong evidence that 75 percent of mergers and acquisitions fail to meet the goal the organizational change was intended to achieve. And a major reason for the 75 percent failure rate? Lack of human involvement in the change effort.

We certainly realize it's not always possible to design the change to involve people and create buy-in, particularly when the change is mandated from above. However, others could be involved in generating ideas on how best to bring about this change—through solution generation. Involvement is one of the primary incentives for those who are motivated to support change. These individuals want to be engaged. If you review the literature and the research on resistance to change, one element comes up over and over again: people who resist a change often have not been involved in planning it. In our own consulting practices, we have talked with managers who have tried to bring about change in their systems, and those managers who failed had not involved others in meaningful ways—whether in the design or the implementation phase, or both.

FACILITATE A MEETING TO HEAR VIEWPOINTS

Consider having a joint session with both resisters and nonresisters present. This stimulates meaningful dialogue and is less likely to segment the group into two camps. During these group sessions, we have often discovered that people need an opportunity to identify some of the losses they are likely to experience, or at least think they are going to experience, such as:

- Loss of identity
- Loss of control
- Loss of meaning
- Loss of belonging
- Loss of competence
- Loss of the future

Remember that resistance to change is often about wrestling with letting go of something that is valued. If you like the staff members with whom you work, for example, and a reorganization pulls you away from your valued colleagues, you will most likely go through a period of grieving. This could entail a range of emotions, depending on your degree of attachment to the group, from frustration to anger. But if you had no particular bond with your work group, your degree of resistance would be minimal.

We suggest that managers listen and read between the lines of what people are saying in relation to these six losses. Resisters may take up significant time; however, they do need to vent, although we strongly recommend that managers limit the time they allow for resisters to express such feelings. Beyond this point, those who continue to resist should be counseled clearly that it is time for them to move forward. If they are not able to do so, propose an honorable exit—an opportunity to look for other options within the organization or termination.

While both resisters and nonresisters are likely to experience these losses, we have found that resisters are more vocal and probably experience their losses much more intensely than do the nonresisters. Examples of each may prove helpful.

Loss of Identity

In response to a change they perceive as affecting them negatively, people who fear loss of identity often ask, "Who am I now?" For example, a doctor might lament, "I was once a surgeon who had complete control over my schedule and was regarded as an independent professional. Now, as an employee of an HMO, I'm just a pawn in the bigger game of hospital politics."

Loss of Control

With this loss, staff members may express feelings such as, "I didn't ask for this. Whose career is this anyway? Who's going to be next on the chopping block? Me?!" This loss is exacerbated when staff members do not have a voice in the change process—that is, when it is done *to* them rather than *with* them. Certainly, everyone cannot be involved with all changes at all stages. But we have rarely seen a change that could not have incorporated some involvement in the process.

Loss of Meaning

In this situation, individuals ask questions like, "Why is this occurring? Why me? Don't my thirty years in this organization count for anything?" What they thought was important to them and to others is seemingly devalued, and they enter a state of confusion and disbelief.

Loss of Belonging

The fourth loss is of belonging. Staff members experiencing this loss may have thoughts such as, "With so many managers running my life, I don't even know who my real boss is anymore." Loss of relationships with others in the organization is the underpinning here. When reorganizations occur, new staff members enter while others leave, and new leaders come on the scene. This kind of loss may be the cause of resistance.

Loss of Competence

People experience this loss when they must acquire a new set of skills in order to meet job expectations. They wonder, "Will I be able to learn the required new skills?" New equipment, technologies, and work processes may pose a threat to individuals who are not confident that they can learn whatever is required. Resistance will be even greater without well-designed training programs that enable staff members to learn new skills.

Loss of the Future

Finally, loss of the future occurs when people feel that their diligence, longevity on the job, and passion for the work are not recognized. They may ask questions such as, "With my great talent and hard work, I should have been promoted by now. Why am I still one of the many?" Change can sometimes mean a staff member's career track and subsequent opportunities will be derailed.

SCENARIO

Dealing with Resistance to Change

Robert is an experienced physician leader in a large midwestern health care organization. For the past three years, his surgical unit has undergone enormous change, including budget constraints, which resulted in surgeons no longer having a choice about the supplies they use, no longer having a say about a focus on increased quality of patient care, and, now, no longer being consulted on a directive from the executive suite that hours of operation must be extended. Robert knows he will meet with strong resistance from most of his medical staff, both surgeons and allied health professionals. He recognizes that he has not always managed change well because of his autocratic style, well developed during his years serving in the U.S. Navy. Robert needs help to develop a strategy that will reduce resistance to the change so that he doesn't lose any valuable staff members. He is most worried that some high-producing surgeons will bolt when faced with a potential extension of their work hours.

Louellen Advises...

Robert, I'd like you to begin by identifying the informal physician leader—someone not in a formal leadership role who has influence with the other physicians—and discuss the pending schedule change with that person. Try to get this person on board with what you are trying to accomplish. Co-opting the opposition and attempting to make this person a collaborator will help you work successfully with the resistance.

Then, develop a strategy for meeting with the physicians first, presenting the change as the solution to a problem that must be resolved. Often, leaders fail to explain the problem a change is designed to fix and therefore give an inadequate explanation of the need. Once the physicians understand the problem, you can then work with them to create a solution to it and emerge with a schedule that best meets their needs.

Next, meet with representatives from the physicians' group and the allied health staff to get their input on the proposed schedule and work collaboratively to meet their needs. It will be crucial to listen carefully and avoid dominating and driving the decision making. I recognize that this may be hard, since you're accustomed to directing your patients' health care, but in this context, put your director's chair to the side! By drawing out and utilizing ideas for the schedule from all parties who will be affected, you will reduce undue resistance. However, if consensus cannot be reached, you may go ahead and develop the schedule relying on the input you have received. It is not always possible to please everyone in a situation like this, so consensus may not be a realistic expectation. If, however, most of the physicians believe that their voices have been heard and that your judgment is sound, you will have enough credibility to drive home the change and overcome the resistance.

Remember this about the change process: Everyone grumbles for a while. If, however, the change turns out to be a good idea, staff members will discover its benefits as it is implemented. Soon, the negativity will dissipate, and you may even begin to hear hints of praise for the new schedule.

Mitch Advises...

In addition to identifying the informal physician leader who has influence with other physicians, as Louellen suggests, I would also urge you to identify a physician who is staunchly resisting the change. I would do this because a fair amount of research evidence strongly suggests that if you can "overturn" a key resister, he or she often becomes your strongest supporter.

I would also like to reinforce the idea of the group collaboratively developing potential solutions to the problem. Involvement has a strong tendency to produce three essential outcomes in any change effort: greater ownership, higher levels of commitment, and more successful results. In terms of decision making, consensus would be the preferred method for you here because professionals want to know their feedback has been heard. If you would like to hear our thoughts regarding the precautions and dilemmas of consensus, we suggest you review our consensus guidelines at the bottom of page 14. The bottom-line message is that consensus does not equal agreement, so you want to be sure to address the criteria in these guidelines and communicate as clearly as possible that you are in a true consensus mode.

My final piece of advice is to ask your team what *you* can do to facilitate change more effectively. Remember, you're known as an autocratic leader and may need to engage the staff, not only in the change itself, but in your efforts to change your directive style. Essentially, Robert, you should be more proactive at walking your talk.

CREATING A CHANGE MANAGEMENT PLAN

Managers are often too haphazard about the way they approach the change process. Eager to implement, they fail to develop plans that provide staff members with clear, consistent direction and communication as a new order is established. Consequently, these managers create a climate of confusion and frustration, which makes the change effort more difficult than is necessary.

A change management plan should be a written document that maps out the route for getting from the current state to the desired state in a well-coordinated manner. Think of it as an anchor that provides some stability for both manager and staff members in the midst of a transition. It is distinct from an operational plan, which outlines goals, strategies for achieving the goals, and action steps for implementing the strategies. A strong change management plan is about the *process* the manager will use to ensure good communication, involvement of staff, and reward and recognition. The following six phases should be included in a well-designed change management plan:

1. Communicating the need for change

2. Involving key stakeholders in creating the change

3. Communicating the change

4. Developing implementation steps

5. Designing communication strategies

6. Creating a reward/recognition mode

Each of these phases is worth further consideration.

PHASE 1: COMMUNICATING THE NEED FOR CHANGE

Many managers do not spend enough time on this phase. In introducing the change, the manager needs to explain what is wrong or ineffective in the current situation so as to create unrest with the status quo, if dissatisfaction does not already exist. This can be done through presentation of data, the telling of stories, or experiences such as focus groups with customers that might sensitize staff to customer service problems.

Let's go into a bit more detail here, because there are many subtle approaches that need to be considered—approaches that may not be evident at first blush. Before describing this process further, we want to point out that we are using the term *phases* rather than *steps*. The reason? *Steps* implies a very concrete and sequential process, which is not completely the case here. Although we suggest a progression from phases 1 through 6, we have found that some phases interact with one another, and, hence, may be difficult to separate. Also, you could get to phase 5, let's say, and then realize that more work needs to be done in phase 2. The phased approach to change reminds the manager to keep in mind the adaptability this kind of fluidity affords. In contrast, steps are quite linear, and there is no up-and-down motion. Therefore, we like to think of this phased process as one that is much more open to critical interaction along the way. For example, the first phase in this change management plan is communicating the need for change, but we see communication as something that should be conducted throughout the entire process. It is indicated here as the first action, not because it is exclusively done first, but because it is the primary focus at this point.

To begin communicating initiation of the change process, we suggest that leaders consider this formula:

$$\text{Dissatisfaction} \times \text{Vision} \times \text{First steps to achieve the vision} > \text{Resistance to change}$$

We borrowed this formula from *Real Time Strategic Change* (1994) by Robert Jacobs, who attributes it to Dick Beckhard, Reuben Harris, and David Gleicher. We have used this formula successfully with hundreds of clients because of its usefulness and simplicity. So, in introducing change—and ultimately communicating it to others—managers need to consider first the *dissatisfaction* with the status quo. Think about it. Since change for the sake of change often fails, people need a reason or rationale for the change effort, and it must mean something to them. The formula is multiplicative. It is simply a means of suggesting that if any of the factors (D, V, or F) is missing, then the product would be essentially zero; consequently, the amount of resistance to change would be greater than the product.

It may be that dissatisfaction already exists. For example, if the change involves restructuring the department, and staff members are pretty much dissatisfied with the way things are working, you may not need to do very much to convince them of the significance of the change effort.

Let's imagine, however, that staff members are totally happy with the current organization and don't want to change. In this circumstance, leaders may actually have to "create" dissatisfaction in the workforce. Before you decide to dump this book in the first available receptacle, hear us out. There must be some motivation for change. Without it, change will be difficult. As the leader, you might try strategies such as asking the staff what would happen to the unit's performance and the team bonus structure after the change is implemented. Or let the staff know that the organizational restructure is the solution you have come up with and invite them to brainstorm an alternative. You could also present compelling facts showing a downward spiral in finances, customer service satisfaction, or quality. Consider appealing to emotions by recounting "horror" stories, for example, of patients who were not well served by current practices, customers who were infuriated by disrespectful behavior, or departments whose work was made more difficult by poor interdepartmental collaboration. Sometimes an audit or an external consultant's assessment is just the thing you need to grab the attention of staff members and get them to accept the need for change.

While creating dissatisfaction with the status quo, leaders should also be pointing out what will remain stable and what will definitely not change (or at least has a low probability of changing). It is important for those affected by the change to understand that there is an anchor in the midst of the seeming chaos, in other words, that not everything is shifting at one time. Leaders must be able to succinctly describe the benefits of change. People need time to discuss the future and, in particular, to understand the principle of WIIFM—*what's in it for me!*

A significant aspect of this stage is that managers must run interference for staff members by reducing potential barriers to successful implementation of the change. All too often, leaders spend an inordinate amount of time preparing for the positive aspects of the change while at the same time neglecting the barriers that could quickly send their change efforts into a tailspin. Therefore, we strongly recommend that managers bring the obstacles out into the open and make some concerted efforts—individually and with the team—to counter these negative forces.

On pages 15–17 we review the vision (*V*) and the first steps (*F*) needed for change.

PHASE 2: INVOLVING KEY STAKEHOLDERS IN CREATING THE CHANGE

A manager may choose, after presenting the need, to have staff members develop ideas for changes that might solve the problem at hand. If the staff is small, the whole group may be involved. If it is large, the manager may choose a representative task force to develop the solutions. In some cases, the change may be dictated by upper management, and the manager could then involve staff members in working on the implementation rather than on the design of the change. Regardless of the specific circumstances, it is crucial that managers involve their staff in every way possible.

Managers sometimes ask us if bringing others in on the change inhibits them in achieving their desired goals because they are, in essence, giving up control. We suggest they employ one of the following processes:

- Seek input alone
- Seek consensus
- Ask the group to tell them how to proceed

Manager Seeks Input Alone

In seeking input, the leader needs to be sure that he or she really listens and makes clear to those participating how their input will be used. At this stage, we would say that a person is better off being an autocratic leader who is honest than a dishonest one who claims to listen to input but really doesn't. If the leader is not able to do what the group suggests, then he or she must explain the rationale for it and be willing to hear other viewpoints before making a final decision.

Manager Seeks Consensus

This is about seeking support, not agreement. The following consensus guidelines may expedite the consensus-seeking process:

1. Define the process for the stakeholders in terms of consensus and a willingness to live with a decision.
2. Place a time parameter around the consensus process. This has been the historical problem with reaching consensus—the process appears to go on indefinitely with no clear end in sight.
3. State how the decision will be made if consensus is not achieved.

There is a fair amount of evidence that consensus really is the preferred mode for group decisions. However, it doesn't always work, and when it doesn't, we recommend that the leader spell out beforehand how the decision will be made in lieu of consensus (e.g., leader decides, majority rule, or most expert person decides). The peril of using an alternative process, such as voting, is that the result may be seen as dividing the group into "winners" and "losers."

Manager Asks How to Proceed

And finally, if the group has greater expertise in the impending change effort, the leader should involve the group in the problem-solving and even design aspects of the change effort. At this stage, either the leader has final control or the group dictates the outcome.

Staff input and the decision-making process should produce a clear understanding of the vision, that is, what the change will look like when complete. Here's where the *V* part of the equation comes into play. We're not talking here about the organization's overall vision or even the vision of the particular department. This will be explored in the context of strategic planning, which we discuss in "Creating an Effective Strategic Planning Process" later in this chapter.

PHASE 3: COMMUNICATING THE CHANGE

Think about your vision of what things will look like when the change is complete and make a concerted effort to communicate it. Consider this. Could you explain a change you are pursuing in two minutes or less to someone who casually asks you what it is and why you are involved in a new initiative? A picture is often worth a thousand words, to use an old cliché. So, for example, if the change involves streamlining a process, make a flowchart that shows the old way of doing things and contrasts it with the new way. If the change involves replacing old software, develop a demonstration of what the new software will do for each person who uses it, showing its features and benefits, and compare it to the old software. The before and after illustrations will make the change as well as its benefits clearer to your staff. In your explanation, emphasize what is in it for them to engage in the change.

PHASE 4: DEVELOPING IMPLEMENTATION STEPS

Once the change is communicated, with the vision being a key stake in the ground, staff members need to know what will happen next. The phases of the change should be delineated with action steps and timelines. For successful implementation of the change effort, leaders need to focus on the *F* in the change formula—the first steps needed to

FIGURE 2. Prioritization Process Matrix—
Resources × Impact

	Few Resources	Some Resources	Many Resources
High Impact			
Medium Impact			
Low Impact			

achieve the vision. These steps should be few in number and represent concrete actions everyone can support. We suggest five to seven.

One of the best strategies we have seen for developing the implementation phase is to find the low-hanging fruit. As indicated by the shaded area of the prioritization process matrix in Figure 2, the implementation effort should start where the impact is highest *and* the least amount of resources is needed. Often, leaders don't break down the implementation steps in this way and begin simply with what is going to produce the greatest impact. We believe in the power of "baby steps" because the best change is one that is well calculated and deliberate and will make a difference. This, in turn, provides the greatest opportunity for people to realize that they can now take on bigger challenges related to the change.

Map out your choices on an action plan and develop a way of monitoring progress. Make sure you don't lose track of what's being done. We have found that creating a visual—online or on the wall—is a great way to do this. When implementation is lengthy, people often begin to lose sight of the end if they don't have a visual representation of what's been done and what's left to accomplish. One of our clients actually created a visual with a large, laminated flowchart and placed it in a public area of the department. The manager encouraged staff members to write their reactions, suggestions, and confusions on the chart. This stimulated three kinds of discussions—informal, online, and in staff meetings. Items were addressed periodically, and those that were resolved were erased from the board. Both the manager and the team affirmed that this visual process got them closer to the ultimate change faster. Craft your own way of making this phase as prominent as possible. Involve your staff in brainstorming some ways to do this. Then follow through with the suggested actions.

PHASE 5: DESIGNING COMMUNICATION STRATEGIES

Next, managers must determine how to communicate updates on the status of the change in a consistent manner. They must determine how to communicate updates, not necessarily do it themselves. This is an important distinction. The leader could create a design team that communicates the strategies, or others may take on this task. Whatever the decision, it is important to assign responsibility for communicating.

Research by John Kotter (1995) of Harvard University has found that leaders undercommunicate by a factor of ten during times of major organizational change! The grapevine then heats up, and misunderstandings abound, creating undue resistance and overreaction. Leaders must establish consistent formal communications in order to overcome this phenomenon. A communication plan should include a schedule of periodic updates, staged frequently enough to keep the gossip under control. E-mail, briefing meetings, broadcast voice mail, podcasts and webcasts, and newsletters are all effective communication tools for keeping staff members well informed. We remember one client—an emergency room management team—that could not communicate messages about impending change to all staff members, given the nature of the work. This led to misunderstanding and resistance based on assumptions and lack of accurate information. The solution to this communication challenge: posting updates on the back of the bathroom stalls, where everyone was sure to go at least once per shift!

PHASE 6: CREATING A REWARD/RECOGNITION MODE

To cap off the change management plan, managers need to develop an approach for consistently recognizing others for their efforts in implementing the change. Lack of recognition often turns a potentially great project into a doomed one. But we caution managers not to think that recognition means the same thing to everyone. For example, for those passionate, innovative, individualistic types—whom we call "mavericks" in our book *Fast Forward Leadership* (Essex and Kusy 1999)—formal recognition programs typically don't work. Recognizing this group with formal celebrations may be a waste of time. Instead, a person in this group would rather have adequate resources to do his or her job or perhaps even an assignment as consultant to a group. This perspective has been validated by a large-scale international study of 4,405 respondents from forty-three companies in sixty-eight countries (McLagan 2003). Mavericks often have the same change profile as that of entrepreneurs. As such, they may not find ongoing support in an organization, particularly when they challenge the status quo. However, they can be helpful in the very first phase of the change management plan—communicating the need for change by creating dissatisfaction with the status quo.

Others may appreciate recognition in the form of a letter to the CEO or president describing the worth of their contribution to the project. At other times, managers could send a simple e-mail informing key stakeholders about the success of the project. We hope you're getting the bottom-line message here—whatever reward you use, tailor it to the needs of the person and the organization.

And don't forget the monetary reward structure. At times, it's important for managers to tie the compensation structure to the change effort. Once the reward system is in place and is associated with the change plan, it is appropriate to assign accountabilities for selected components of the plan.

SCENARIO

Developing a Change Management Plan

Janet is in the midst of reorganizing her accounts receivable department, which is part of an international cereal-manufacturing company. She has developed a team-based structure that will assign teams of staff members to groups of clients, based on geographic location. This will require staff members to work more collaboratively than ever before. They will also have to establish relationships with other clients and leave behind some with whom they have worked for many years. Janet wants to create a process that will promote staff buy-in but doesn't quite know where to begin. It seems as if most managers in her organization simply dictate a change each step of the way, but she has observed that the result is usually lowered morale and productivity. She knows that change could be an energizing experience for staff if she adopts the right leadership strategies. But what are they, and how should she proceed?

Mitch Advises...

Before you do anything, Janet, I recommend bringing all staff members together and explaining some of the current dilemmas that indicate the need for change (e.g., geographically dispersed teams that need to be much more collaborative). In doing this, you provide your assessment of the situation. You should also invite others on your staff to express their own thoughts in a brainstorming format. Then, after a brief period of time, I suggest you have the group collapse these brainstormed items into a very small number of themes. Place these on a matrix (like the one shown in Figure 2); select the ones that emerge as high priority (having high impact but requiring few resources) for action. Then proceed with the change formula we discussed in this chapter: $D \times V \times F > R$. Identify dissatisfactions with the status quo, provide a vision to address these, and complete the process with the first steps needed to achieve the vision for each item in the shaded area of the matrix. This should reduce the probability of significant resistance to change as well as enhance the success of your change effort.

Louellen Advises...

Janet, in communicating the need for the change, you must be clear about what's wrong with the way things are now. In other words, create dissatisfaction with the status quo, recognizing that some staff members are wedded to the existing structure and most likely don't see any reason for change. You will need to create some tension in order to stimulate the momentum toward change.

Next, engage your staff in the process of brainstorming and initial planning, making sure to develop a written document describing the action steps, persons responsible, and timelines for execution. Work diligently to make sure things get done and staff can clearly see that progress is being made. You and the staff could easily lose track of the action steps that have been completed, resulting in confusion and discouragement. You may want to consider using online project management tools to help you stay disciplined about tracking the implementation plan. Create a way for staff members to coach one another on how to deal most effectively with the clients they know best. That way, you won't lose the wisdom inherent in the current set of relationships.

Now the fun part. Reward and recognize after each milestone is met, using a creative array of methods—awards, parties, gift giving, storytelling, thank-yous, and acknowledgment of special talents staff members displayed. Think of this as *managing the mood*. When you notice that negativity is setting in, intervene by talking with your staff members, individually and collectively. Infuse energy and offer recognition to lift the mood and instill hope that the change is making a difference. And, Janet, don't forget to take care of yourself. No one needs a cranky manager during times of stressful change!

CREATING AN EFFECTIVE STRATEGIC PLANNING PROCESS

Often short-staffed and underfunded, managers are driven to focus on operational concerns—getting through each day, meeting short-term objectives, and just staying afloat. While it may appear this is the only way to survive, the opposite is really true. If an organization doesn't take the long view, it may die a slow death, becoming irrelevant or being overtaken by a savvier competitor.

The process for strategic planning typically encompasses several phases, which we summarize here (Kusy and McBain 2000). As you review this process, we suggest that you not approach it as the definitive way to do strategic planning but rather as just one model. We have found it effective, but you will need to adapt it to your group's needs. For example, your team may already understand its purpose or mission, so it won't be necessary to go through a phase of formal mission development. There are many iterations of the basic strategic planning process. You may want to consider adapting it to the needs of your own team.

1. Planning to plan

2. Scanning

3. Mission focus

4. Vision creation

5. Goal development

6. Strategy formulation

7. Action planning and follow-up

Now, let's examine each of these phases in detail.

PHASE 1: PLANNING TO PLAN

In this phase, the leader sets the stage for the planning effort by determining logistics, such as who needs to be involved, how long the planning process should take, and even how decisions will be made during the planning process. The planning-to-plan process should include development of planning assumptions that specify the criteria for creating boundaries around the strategic planning process.

Begin by inviting a small representative group from within your team. This group is not necessarily the leadership team, and nonleaders should also be among those participating. Some people call this the "steering committee" or the "planning committee." Whatever you decide to call it, it's most important to make sure that this group understands its goal, which is not to design strategy but rather to design the process for others (including members of this team), all of whom will ultimately design the strategy.

TABLE 1. Questions to Ask in the Planning-to-Plan Phase

Questions	Examples
What does the leader and/or the planning-to-plan team want to accomplish with the strategic planning process?	• Articulate a mission • Create a three-year vision • Create a five-year vision • Develop an action plan for the future • Determine whether anything from the previous strategic planning effort (if there is one) needs to be revised
Who should be involved?	• Management • Staff and management • A sample of volunteers or a randomly selected group
What amount of time, realistically, is available for strategic planning?	• Hours • Days • Weeks
What is the decision-making vehicle?	• Management receives input and decides • Consensus between management and staff • Majority rule
What are the parameters of the strategic planning process?	• What is off-limits? • What must be done without discussion?

The leader of the team may decide to facilitate this group or assign the responsibility to a person with strong facilitation skills. This is also an excellent opportunity for someone who would like to develop additional facilitation skills as part of his or her career development, with the leader serving as a coach on the side. Table 1 provides several examples of questions leaders should consider during the planning-to-plan phase.

Much of what you see in Table 1 is self-explanatory. But leaders sometimes overlook one aspect—the power of involving others, including those from outside management ranks. The traditional or archaic way of conducting strategic planning is to involve just those in management ranks. Please keep in mind that the involvement of others, including nonmanagement staff, significantly increases the probability of greater ownership of the plan, better results, and higher levels of commitment to it.

Most managers fear that by involving others in the strategic planning process, they will raise expectations and then not be able to do what people suggest. First, we recommend letting participants know the boundaries of what can and can't be done. For example, perhaps costs must be reduced by 5 percent, no new staff can be hired, or the proposed day-care facility must wait another year. Second, determine the types of decisions that will derive from strategic planning made via consensus, majority rule, or input from staff members to leaders. Make sure you define these decision-making models clearly. For example, remind people that consensus is about support of, not necessarily agreement with, a decision. Majority rule tends to divide the group into those who "won" and those who "lost," so be careful of this one! Input is fine as long as the leader or leadership team intends to really listen and at least explain how the input was used in the decision-making process.

PHASE 2: SCANNING

Scanning should begin with an analysis of the trends—societal, financial, political, community-wide, industry-wide—that may affect the organization doing the planning. This is just a very short list of criteria for evaluating trends. As part of this scanning process, group members determine what they believe is most important for trend analysis. After analyzing the trends, the planning team must make some assumptions about the future, which should encompass what they believe to be their "best bets."

Next, group members conduct a SWOT analysis. The key to the SWOT analysis, which we know many of you have heard about and perhaps even done, is that it must be both an internal and an external assessment—internal via understanding the team's strengths (S) and weaknesses (W), and external via understanding the team's opportunities (O) and threats (T). Sometimes an organization spends far too much time on the analysis and ends up losing the group's interest. We suggest keeping it brief and quickly moving through a brainstorming mode. It really is not necessary to arrive at consensus on the top items in each category. Rather, brainstorming will result in a list that spurs creative thinking in areas participants may not have thought much about. If there's time, the leader certainly may facilitate consensus around the themes in each category. This is up to the leader and the team.

PHASE 3: MISSION FOCUS

In this phase, the leader works with the team to encapsulate the overall purpose. The mission is enduring—something that typically does not change over time, unless there is a crisis or major organization-altering event.

In working with clients in the strategic planning arena, we have seen that more misunderstandings occur around the terms *mission* and *vision* than around most other terms used. We see the mission as the team's or the organization's purpose; vision is its direction. In fact, we have found that using the terms *purpose* for the mission and *direction* for the vision reduces confusion. In this phase of strategic planning, the team comes to consensus on its purpose—why it exists. The description should be brief, fifteen words or less.

Here's a summary, based on our own experiences, of what every team mission needs to be:

- Connected with the larger organization's mission by supporting it

- Capable of encapsulating the purpose of your team, department, or unit

- Relatively enduring, so that there is low probability it will change frequently over time

PHASE 4: VISION CREATION

Vision is a team's or organization's desired direction for a specified period of time. It is the preferred future—the ideal. Most organizations assume a three- to five-year direction, but a few go as far out as ten years. We have found the most success with visions that are three to five years in length. Much less than three years tends to make the strategic planning process too operational; more than five years is too much like science fiction. Like the mission statement, the statement of direction should be brief, fifteen words or less, and powerful in its language.

In order to make the vision more than just a statement, we suggest integrating it with the organization's performance management system. For example, if a team member is doing something that really contributes to the organization's direction, the leader should acknowledge this behavior to the person. Let's say an individual is effectively coaching a team member. The leader could share how this person's coaching behavior relates to achievement of the vision and also how he or she is moving the organization just a bit closer to achieving its vision through these coaching actions. Similarly, if someone is doing something counterproductive, the leader should have a performance discussion with the individual and share with him or her precisely how that performance is inhibiting achievement of the vision.

In our view, a good vision does the following:

- Challenges and inspires

- Focuses on something that is attainable

- Is associated with the purpose of the team/organization

- Builds on a three- to five-year direction

- Provides a base for goal development

Much of this is common sense. However, so many organizations go overboard and create directions that are esoteric, long, and ultimately meaningless. What's yours like? Does it go on too long? Is it on a plaque that no one reads? Table 2 provides some examples of good vision statements.

PHASE 5: GOAL DEVELOPMENT

At this point, you are ready to determine your broad goals for the next three- to five-year period. Keep these goals concrete and not too many in number; we recommend no more than five to six broad goals. For those

TABLE 2. Sample Vision Statements from Selected Organizations

We make a difference to New Zealand by making the desirable affordable.

To make a contribution to the world that advances humankind.

To preserve and improve human life.

To encourage and develop leadership skills for the good of society overall.

Merge economic growth with social responsibility.

Make sure that journalistic excellence and profitability go hand in hand.

Find a way to use the entrepreneurial energy and the fast pace of a new economy to kick-start an old-economy giant.

Create hundreds of small entrepreneurial businesses that come together to make one big business.

leaders who question this number, consider this statistic: Jack Welch, famed former CEO of GE, initiated only six major organizational change goals in his eighteen years at GE. That's approximately one change goal every three years!

To identify no more than six goals, have the group brainstorm and then prioritize. Use the following step-by-step process as a template:

1. Brainstorm all the goals that must be met to achieve the vision.

2. Eliminate redundancies in the brainstormed list.

3. Number each of the brainstormed items sequentially, not according to priority.

4. Ask each participant to determine individually whether the group's current performance on each goal is low, medium, or high and whether the importance of each goal is low, medium, or high.

5. Duplicate the matrix in Figure 3 and enlarge it (e.g., 2 feet by 3 feet) so that everyone can see it from a distance. Ask each person to either write the goal number in the corresponding area of the

FIGURE 3. Prioritization Process Matrix—
Performance × Importance

	Low Performance	Medium Performance	High Performance
High Importance	G	H	I
Medium Importance	D	E	F
Low Importance	A	B	C

graph (A, B, C, D, E, F, G, H, or I) or write the number on a Post-It and place the Post-It on the graph.

6. The planning-to-plan team then meets while the other group members take a break from their individual prioritization process. The team counts the goals in each category and shares the results with the entire group.

7. The group arrives at consensus on no more than six goals in the category of **low performance × high importance** (category G in Figure 3). If there are more than six, the team works and reworks the goals until they are reduced to no more than six.

PHASE 6: STRATEGY FORMULATION

How will you achieve each of these prioritized goals? Your choice of method becomes your strategy. Here's where careful analysis and creativity come into play. Let's use a personal example in order to understand this more fully. If you decide your goal is to lose twenty-five pounds, you need to determine strategies for accomplishing this goal. There are thousands of weight loss strategies. As you analyze yourself and your lifestyle, the best strategy for your situation emerges. Perhaps you are very social and respond well to peer pressure. Maybe you are data oriented and like to work with facts. So a point-based, group-oriented approach to weight loss, like Weight Watchers, might be your best strategy.

In enacting this step in an organizational setting, your internal and external scan should be the means by which you filter alternatives. If the trends suggest you will have a talent shortage within three years, then you will need a strategy to offset problems in recruiting and maintaining high-quality staff members who will be able to support your goals. You might look to hiring part-time workers or retirees, or developing a work climate attractive to young superstars. Or you might decide on an entirely different strategy, such as investing in more technology that will reduce the need for staff.

PHASE 7: ACTION PLANNING AND FOLLOW-UP

In this last phase, you develop the specific actions you and your staff will take to reach each of the strategies associated with the goals. Establish a completion date and assign responsibility. You can't have actions but no people associated with coordinating them. Assign a coordinator to each action step or solicit volunteers for this role. We recently consulted with one large law firm that had been through similar strategic planning in the past and found it to be largely a waste of time. So we suggested that the leader assign a coordinator to each of the strategies. Because law firms thrive on billable time, what this organization did was unprecedented in the legal profession. The leader reduced the billable hours for every attorney who agreed to coordinate a strategy. Essentially, each attorney's workload was reduced. John Kotter (1995) has stated that you can't keep adding new assignments to an already overloaded schedule. We concur. The process at this law firm was highly successful.

Follow-up consists of these coordinators meeting with their teams regularly and with the other coordinators on a consistent basis. Remember that effective follow-up is not just for those who attended the event but for anyone who has a stake in the success of this plan. For these coordinators, the key is to communicate, communicate, communicate. Remember to have coordinators ask stakeholders for their input as important messages are communicated. To ensure consistent communication, consider developing a visual timeline—online or on the wall. Then, check off each step as it is completed, so that all involved can see that progress is being made.

SCENARIO

Developing a Change Management Process

Sarah has been managing the community service division of a large nonprofit agency for two years. It has become apparent to her that the organization within which she works is quite reactive, responding to requests for new services as they are initiated by the board of directors while maintaining and attempting to strengthen current programs each year. Sarah worries, though, that change is occurring rapidly in the community, with new needs, as well as competing agencies, emerging every day. Since funding is limited, and most of it must be obtained through grants and donations, Sarah believes the organization needs to think more strategically. But what does that really mean? She wants to take the lead in influencing the executive director, board of directors, and other managers to embark on a strategic planning process that will set the course for the next three to five years. She needs help preparing her proposal, outlining the rationale for strategic planning, and implementing the process.

Louellen Advises...

OK, Sarah, you have a critical leadership opportunity facing you. By looking at the future of the organization, you are stepping out of your daily management role and assuming a leadership role. Good for you! Clearly, your organization could be on the path to disaster if it does not develop a strategic focus. Prepare an overview of the strategic planning process for your executive director. Complete a draft of the external scan, demonstrating that trends clearly indicate your organization needs to create a new way of doing things. Show how the competition for funding is heating up, how the client profile is changing, how the method of service delivery is becoming obsolete—any argument you think will capture the executive director's attention. Be clear and concise and present the information assertively. Think, too, about who you would suggest should be involved in the planning effort. While it may, at first glance, look like something the board and management team should produce, consider crafting a strategic planning group that also includes staff representation. This will set the stage for more buy-in from those who will have to implement the plan.

Increasingly organizations are using large-scale planning processes. This means that everyone in the organization participates in at least part of the planning effort. Recently, I facilitated a planning event with a regional medical center that involved 250 staff members from all levels of the organization. They sat at tables of twelve—maintenance staff alongside physicians and administrators—creating pictures and words describing their preferred vision for the future of the medical center. We provided some information on relevant trends (the result of internal and external scanning) to stimulate their thinking. Then a smaller representative group of thirty developed a vision statement and accompanying goals. It was a big success and was greatly appreciated by everyone, many of whom had never participated in creating the organization's future.

So move quickly! Your organization needs your insight and plan of action.

Mitch Advises...

The very first thing I suggest you do, Sarah, is form the planning-to-plan team. This will give you some insights into both the content needed for strategic planning and the process required for accomplishing the plan. Ask who would like to be on the team. Also seek those who are resisting this effort, because if you can turn around a resister, that person may become your best ally. Once you have assembled this team, go through Table 1 (page 22) and have the team discuss various planning-to-plan criteria. Pay close attention to any push-back from management, which may want to do it themselves and not involve others or may want to involve others in minimal ways (e.g., by deciding to share the plan only when it's done). Don't go along with it. Yes, this engaged process will take longer, but the end result will be far more successful and productive. Be sure to address the SWOT analysis and pay special attention to the external components (opportunities and threats), as these are most likely to affect your team's success, given the external competition in your industry. Let the team know that this competition is highly significant and that there could be tremendous benefit from having a goal that relates to this variable.

CHAPTER 2

Building Collaboration and Teamwork

TEAM: **T**OGETHER **E**VERYONE **A**CHIEVES **M**ORE. You may have seen this plastered on walls in conference rooms, office cubicles, hallways, and maybe even your manager's office. While the slogan's sentiment seems obvious, the ability to instill a collaborative spirit in the mind-set of each staff person is a daunting challenge for any leader. Today's work environments require collaboration within and across work units in order to ensure smooth and efficient operations, yet many individuals seem to focus only on their own needs, sometimes at the expense of group performance. So how does a leader harness the individualistic, competitive spirit of some and develop collaboration and teamwork so as to achieve collective outcomes?

In this chapter, we share our best strategies for building collaboration in three venues:

- Within a work unit
- Within a cross-functional team comprising members from different work units
- Across multiple work units

Then we give you some designs for facilitating a team-building session that will work in any of those venues. The goal of this chapter is to provide you with hands-on approaches that consultants use to add significant value to what teams already do.

But first, we should explain that, in our experience, when *any* of those groups goes awry, the range of dysfunctional behaviors demonstrated is virtually the same:

- Minimal communication occurs between team members, which results in hoarding of information.

- Team members do not trust one another or the leader.

- Team members make excessive negative assumptions about the intent behind the behavior of others on the team.

- The team dynamic is characterized by polarization, with cliques often forming.

- Interpersonal conflict between team members remains unresolved and/or exaggerated.

- Team members view and execute their roles rigidly, with little willingness to be flexible.

- The team experiences low productivity; individuals may be performing but not nearly as effectively as if the team were truly functional.

- Expected outcomes for individuals and the team are ill-defined or ignored.

- Mechanisms for individual and team accountability are few.

A leader must act quickly to reduce the intensity or frequency of these unproductive patterns.

By contrast, great teams are characterized by the opposite behaviors. They have clear goals and roles, a well-defined strategy for working together, high respect for the styles and talents of other team members, and a high performance–oriented culture. To explore this further, complete Exercise 1, Teamability Assessment. Note that each question provides details on an element of effective teamwork. If you want to conduct a more comprehensive assessment, ask team members to complete the survey as well and hold a meeting to discuss results. Then plan to make the necessary changes and capitalize on what you are doing well.

EXERCISE 1. Teamability Assessment

Directions: Rate your team on the following scale by circling the number to the right of the statement that corresponds best to your views:

1 = Strongly disagree (SD)   **4** = Agree (A)

2 = Disagree (D)   **5** = Strongly agree (SA)

3 = Unsure (U)

	SD	D	U	A	SA
1. We have clear goals. *Comments:*	1	2	3	4	5
2. We have challenging team-performance standards. *Comments:*	1	2	3	4	5
3. Team members' roles have been clearly defined. *Comments:*	1	2	3	4	5
4. Team members' skills are complementary. *Comments:*	1	2	3	4	5
5. We have established team guidelines/norms for how we want to work together. *Comments:*	1	2	3	4	5
6. We have taken time to build relationships through activities that help us to know one another better. *Comments:*	1	2	3	4	5
7. Communication among team members is open, allowing for free flow of information in a timely manner. *Comments:*	1	2	3	4	5

	SD	D	U	A	SA
8. Conflict between individuals typically gets resolved. *Comments:*	1	2	3	4	5
9. Our team meetings are productive. *Comments:*	1	2	3	4	5
10. We encourage all team members to express their ideas. *Comments:*	1	2	3	4	5
11. We approach problem solving by looking at a wide range of alternatives and then selecting the best based on objective analysis. *Comments:*	1	2	3	4	5
12. Team members trust each other. *Comments:*	1	2	3	4	5
13. We organize tasks well. *Comments:*	1	2	3	4	5
14. We demonstrate creativity in our approach to doing work. *Comments:*	1	2	3	4	5
15. We have established a way of measuring our progress on goals. *Comments:*	1	2	3	4	5

EXERCISE 1 *cont'd*

	SD	D	U	A	SA
16. We regularly celebrate our accomplishments. *Comments:*	1	2	3	4	5
17. We are recognized by the organization for our work. *Comments:*	1	2	3	4	5
18. We regularly evaluate our team performance. *Comments:*	1	2	3	4	5
19. We work well with others in our organization. *Comments:*	1	2	3	4	5

From your perspective, what are your team's greatest strengths?

How do you think your team could be more effective?

If you could change one thing about your team, what would it be?

Additional comments:

Source: Louellen Essex & Associates, 2004

BUILDING COLLABORATION
WITHIN A WORK UNIT

Of the three team venues, everyone is probably most attuned to the one that consists of members from the same work unit. This venue is often referred to as the "intact team." In all likelihood, we have all worked in this situation, with achievement levels ranging from highly productive to downright dismal. At the less productive end of this continuum, a team sometimes exhibits classic symptoms of dysfunctional behavior, and it's here that the leader must respond with methods to restore the group's effectiveness. Without intervention, there will most likely be further disintegration and loss of the ability to work together effectively. The flowchart in Figure 4 will help any leader determine the red flag behaviors that must be addressed to build the team's strength.

It's important to recognize that not all work units must function as a close-knit team. Sometimes a basic level of cooperation is all that is needed—willingness to back one another up when necessary, share certain types of information, and provide emotional support when problems arise. When team members perform tasks relatively independently, this mode may be appropriate. In other cases, the level of teamwork may require group problem solving and decision making, constant communication among team members, and high levels of interdependency. This is when team-building activities will be most helpful.

TEAM'S LEVEL OF DYSFUNCTION

First, every leader needs to determine how poorly the team is functioning. If it has been dysfunctional for a long time, to the point that people don't even want to be around one another, and has been volatile in that outbursts are the common form of communication, we strongly suggest you forget about team building. Clients who have consulted us in this kind of situation have said that disaster ensued when they attempted a team intervention, either solo or with a consultant. This scenario has given team building a very bad reputation over the years, and many leaders and team members think of team building somewhat dismis-

FIGURE 4. Flowchart for Improving Teamwork

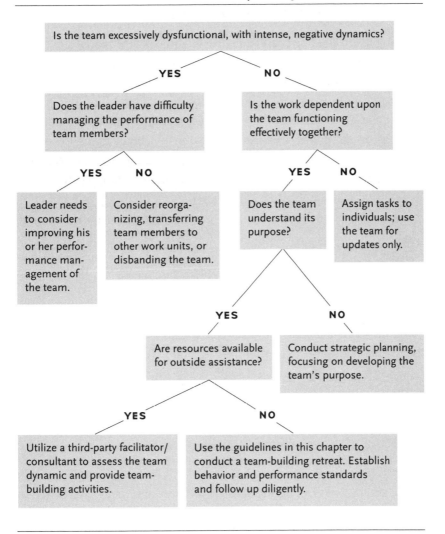

Is the team excessively dysfunctional, with intense, negative dynamics?

YES — Does the leader have difficulty managing the performance of team members?

NO — Is the work dependent upon the team functioning effectively together?

YES — Leader needs to consider improving his or her performance management of the team.

NO — Consider reorganizing, transferring team members to other work units, or disbanding the team.

YES — Does the team understand its purpose?

NO — Assign tasks to individuals; use the team for updates only.

YES — Are resources available for outside assistance?

NO — Conduct strategic planning, focusing on developing the team's purpose.

YES — Utilize a third-party facilitator/consultant to assess the team dynamic and provide team-building activities.

NO — Use the guidelines in this chapter to conduct a team-building retreat. Establish behavior and performance standards and follow up diligently.

sively as "games" and "exercises." This form of action, though, does have a place. When applied in the right context, team building can be highly successful in producing dramatically improved outcomes. Like a good antibiotic, team building will work effectively in selected situations. And if it's going to work, you'll know in a very short period of time.

DIFFICULTY MANAGING THE PERFORMANCE OF TEAM MEMBERS

Moving down the flowchart in Figure 4, you will see that, if the team is dysfunctional, the first question is, "Does the leader have difficulty managing the performance of team members?" This is a critical question because, in our experience, we have found that team building should not be the intervention if there is a leader problem. We can't state this strongly enough. We have heard from so many clients trying to do team building when the real issue is the leader needing to be a better manager of the performance of others. While there certainly can be team issues that occur because of the leader's lack of ability, consider first whether the leader needs to improve his or her performance management skills. Once this happens, the leader can proceed through the flowchart and determine whether or not team building is appropriate. The bottom line here is that leaders need to get their house in order before inviting guests to join the banquet! (For more on how to manage a team's performance, see Chapter 3.)

If the team is intensely dysfunctional, and the leader has not had difficulty managing the performance of group members, team building is again not the step to take. Instead, we recommend any one of three actions:

- Reorganizing
- Transferring team members to other work units
- Disbanding the team

None should be taken lightly because all three are major calls to action.

Reorganizing

While we have seen reorganization overused, this action does have its place. Specifically in this context, reorganization works because it provides opportunities for team members to start anew without the excess baggage of old team dynamics. However, the primary reason for the reorganization should be not to ignore team problems but to help members become more productive. The leader should initiate a reorganization with the bottom-line message that its goal is to improve the group's interdependence, the sine qua non for greater productivity.

Transferring Team Members to Other Work Units

Reorganization, though, is quite disruptive and should be used only when other, more moderate actions, such as transferring team members to other work units, won't work. Be careful with this one! Transferring individuals doesn't uproot the entire team as a reorganization would, but it could blow up in your face if you do not consider some important variables.

If you believe that the team's makeup is a key variable in its success or failure, moving individuals elsewhere may work. However, this action is effective only if a different environment will be healthier for the team members you transfer. We have also found that the leader should do some preliminary work. For example, members of a team that will be receiving a new member need assistance in understanding how the additional person will add value. And there are likely to be the ever-present rumors about the reasons for the transfer. It's best to be honest and direct with that team in this circumstance. If the dynamics are evident to all, don't pretend. You might say, for example, "There were some significant issues on this team, and I'd like to provide a new environment for this individual," or "I know this team has been very accepting of new members in the past, and I'd like to engage you in doing this again with an unproductive situation in another team." Be careful not to blame the other team. You could phrase it this way: "We all know that, in *any* team, there can be dynamics that simply don't work. But new environments can be rejuvenating. So let's welcome Sally to this team and provide an environment that will really work for all."

Disbanding the Team

Finally, the leader may consider disbanding the team if its dynamics are really dysfunctional *and* the team is no longer needed. As we noted above, there are alternatives to try before turning to this intervention. Interestingly, as consultants, we have discovered that leaders hang on to the idea that teams are always needed. Not so! When you disband the team, let the members know why. If it's only because the group is dysfunctional, that is not enough reason, and you should consider the other interventions we have already described. However, if the team is dysfunctional *and* the work can be done in other ways, find those alternative means and disband the group. Let team members know how you plan to cover their former team's responsibilities.

WORK DEPENDENT ON TEAM FUNCTIONING

Now, let's consider the right-hand side of the flowchart in Figure 4, where the team has not been intensely dysfunctional for a long period of time. In this event, the first question is, "Is the work dependent upon the team functioning effectively together?" If the answer is yes, then there is one action to be considered. This action relates to the team's purpose.

Developing the Team's Purpose

In the hundreds of team-building consultations we have facilitated, the number one variable we consider is the team's purpose or mission. This experience is validated by many research studies demonstrating that the group needs to understand why it exists before anything is done to improve its functioning. Makes sense, right? We think so. However, an inordinate number of the many team-building actions organizations run focus exclusively on relationship building. While this is important, there are other factors to consider as well.

Carl Larson and Frank LaFasto (1989) conducted an outstanding study of seventy-five teams across the United States. These included cardiovascular surgery units, mountain-climbing teams, groups from the Centers for Disease Control, the IBM PC unit, the 1966 Notre Dame championship football team, management and executive groups, and even the McDonald's Chicken McNuggets team! The researchers discovered that one distinct variable contributed to the teams' successes— they had a single clear, elevating goal, an overriding sense of purpose. And what got in the way of effectiveness? Larson and LaFasto found that when individual success took precedence over the team's success, productivity plummeted.

We take this research to heart. So much so that whenever we are called in to consult on a team's functioning and there's a possibility of engaging in team building, the first thing we look for is whether the team has a sense of purpose or, in other words, a clear elevating goal. Then we investigate further by examining whether team members operate under this sense of purpose. So before beginning any intervention, be sure you, as the leader, engage the team in understanding and acting upon its purpose or mission. For more on this perspective, review the section on mission focus in Chapter 1.

Establishing Behavior and Performance Standards

If the team has a purpose or mission and understands it, you can focus the team-building effort on behavior and performance standards. Teams are critical when collaboration is needed to produce the most effective work product or service. In order to establish collaboration, you, as the leader, must clarify group performance standards and accountabilities for the team and for individuals. This might entail, for example, an output number (claims processed, calls handled, problems solved, and so on). In a service, educational, health, government, or other nonprofit organization, it could be assessment of how effectively clients are being serviced, how well student concerns are being addressed, or how satisfied patients are with the service they have received. A superb exercise for any team is to brainstorm how some "soft" behaviors can be translated into something more concrete and measurable.

We also suggest that you involve team members in reaching consensus on the top measurable outcomes on which they would like to focus their energy. Be careful not to select more than five. The fewer, the better, so that each can receive enough attention. Once these outcomes are identified, we recommend involving the team in designing systems for measuring them. Methods may include, for example, focus groups made up of a select group of clients, analysis of the percentage of students who have gained entry to colleges, or surveys identifying patient satisfaction. Whatever you determine as the outcome, there should be a strong association between it and the measurement system. Something else to consider here: Your organization may already have some measurement process built into other systems. So, as an alternative activity, you might send team members on a "scavenger hunt" to find these processes and devise ways of applying them to the outcomes. We hope you're starting to see team building as a truly outcome-based activity, not one that is "soft" in nature.

Team members also need to determine how they are going to contribute to these new measurable outcomes. Ask them to provide details on the following key commitments:

- Specific behaviors they will contribute to the outcome(s)

- Help or support they might need from others to do this

- What they will do if they get stuck in the process

We suggest that you document the responses, send them out the next day via e-mail, and reconvene within two weeks to check on progress. And, when appropriate, leaders may also want to contribute their own commitments, as related to the outcomes their teams have spelled out.

Please note that these are the individual behaviors needed to support the team's new outcomes. Likewise, team members should follow a similar process to identify the collaborative processes necessary to achieve the outcomes. They may wish to come up with a charter, or ground rules, stating the team-oriented behaviors they will adopt in support of the new outcomes. For example, team members may pledge to talk directly to individuals about conflicts or concerns rather than talking about them behind their back. Or they may decide to stipulate that individuals should inform the group ahead of time when they can't meet specific deadlines as well as seek assistance in advance. You probably get the drift here. This exercise can also be very useful for identifying future new norms.

Rewards and Recognition

And don't forget the significance of rewards, which the leader should establish for team outcomes. As we noted previously, it's key to brainstorm some team rewards and then distill this list into a smaller group of items that really mean something to people. Let the team have some fun with this. You'll probably discover reward items you never even thought of. Likewise for consequences . . . let the team brainstorm these and then identify a condensed list—both positive and negative. Positive consequences may include items such as more team respect throughout the organization, greater productivity, and a more enjoyable working environment. Negative consequences could include reduction in annual bonuses for individuals who do not live up to their commitments.

SCENARIO

Promoting Team Collaboration Within a Work Unit

Melissa, a marketing manager for a midsize food company, is worried about her work unit. Increasingly, its members have engaged in conflict over what she views as petty arguments, passive-aggressive retaliation, and "unfinished" business. Now the team is split into two factions. Productivity and creativity have slumped, as more energy seems to go into squabbling than into producing good work. Team members are working independently and seem to avoid communicating with one another. She has attempted to talk with them as a whole group about the need for better teamwork, but nothing changes. Each faction has a ringleader who does an excellent job of keeping the pot stirred. She wonders what she can do to pull the team together again and create a collaborative environment.

Mitch Advises...

This is a prime example of what happens when the leader doesn't manage performance effectively. As we said earlier, never do team building if there's a leadership issue. It appears to me that you may not have been doing an effective job of managing the team's performance. Therefore, I suggest you do an about-face and start setting performance parameters—essentially, what is expected and the consequences for both meeting them and not meeting them. Melissa, you may want to consider doing this in the following ways:

1. Let staff know that performance parameters will be set.

2. Define these performance expectations for the team, including which behaviors will not be tolerated and the consequences for each.

3. Facilitate a team-building session in which team members determine:

    - Specific behaviors each will adopt so as to contribute to the new performance expectations

    - What help or support each might need from others in order to do this

    - What each team member will do if he or she gets stuck in the process

4. And finally—ending on a positive note—follow up one week later, find some positives for each team member, and share the good news with the team. A couple of weeks later, gather the group and have them do the same thing.

Louellen Advises...

You've got your hands full, Melissa. I'm going to guess that you have been a little lax in holding the group to performance standards, and now things are getting out of hand. Keep in mind that not all adults behave well in the absence of limits. Meet with your team and lay down the law, using a little bit of tough love. Tell them what you've observed, the negative outcomes of their behavior, and ask them to join you in setting new ground rules for interaction. Define what collaboration means within your work unit and what it looks like when team members engage in it. Don't assume they know what you are talking about when you use the word *teamwork*. Ask for each staff member's commitment and follow up with monthly meetings to track progress. Then reward, reward, reward.

Another important consideration is to be sure the team has a clear purpose and that everyone understands what it is. If they do, define measurable goals and provide the accompanying metrics. Then, taking work-related examples, determine the roles each team member would play in achieving them. I've often found that the disruptive behavior you are encountering, Melissa, is a symptom of a deeper problem: the lack of a purpose that is understood and agreed upon by all team members.

If your effort is not as successful as you would like, consider bringing in a third party to assist. A consultant, internal or external, could conduct confidential interviews with each staff member and prepare a report of the findings. The report could then be shared with staff members as a way of raising their awareness of the problems and sharing the consultant's view of what they need to do to be more effective. Sometimes a person who is perceived as more neutral can be a better facilitator in this type of situation, freeing you to listen, observe, and participate.

BUILDING COLLABORATION WITHIN A CROSS-FUNCTIONAL TEAM

The cross-functional team is virtually an everyday phenomenon in organizations today. Here, staff from different units form an ad hoc team for the purpose of accomplishing a specific project within the organization. Typically, this kind of team disbands once the assignment is accomplished, unlike the work-unit team, which often continues beyond any one project. With cross-functional teamwork, creating a smooth flow of activity coupled with effective communication does not happen easily. By nature, work units tend to protect their domains and quickly establish an "us vs. them" posture. In *Fast Forward Leadership* (Essex and Kusy 1999), we discuss the dynamics of competition, wherein individuals fail to share information and close themselves off in a silo. We contrast this with the dynamics of cooperation, which are more fluid and open, characterized by team members who are eager to learn from one another by entertaining new ideas from sources outside their immediate work arenas. Leaders need to help cross-functional team members make this transition, from a work-unit team to a work group with members from several units within the leader's domain.

Figure 5 illustrates the dimensions needed to build cross-functional collaboration. First, it must be clear that the overriding goal of the team requires interdependency among the functions or roles represented. If

FIGURE 5. Flowchart for Improving
Cross-Functional Teamwork

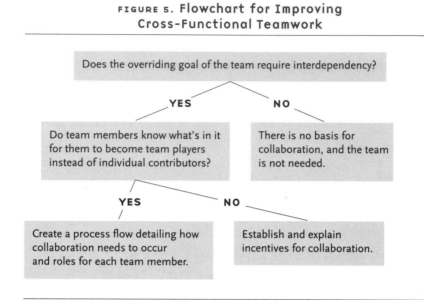

not, there is no basis for collaboration. Second, team members must know the personal benefits of becoming team players rather than remaining individual contributors. A reward structure focused on collaborative outcomes, with diminished recognition for individualistic behavior, will fuel team spirit. Third, the team must create a process flow, detailing how collaboration needs to occur, by asking the following questions:

- What are the phases we must work through so as to achieve the desired result?

- At what points will we make decisions together, and what decisions can be made by individuals with or without input from the group?

- What are our expectations of one another regarding communication (timeliness, content, mode, frequency)?

- How and when will we evaluate the effectiveness of our team process and outcomes?

- Who needs to approve our work, and at what points in the process do we seek approval?

These same questions could come up within a work-unit team, but they are definitely intensified in the cross-functional team. One of the most obvious reasons is that several managers oversee the work of individual members on the cross-functional team. The critical question becomes, Who is holding team members accountable?

COMMUNICATION STRATEGIES
FOR THE CROSS-FUNCTIONAL TEAM

While each manager should ensure that staff members from his or her area are meeting expectations, it is often particularly useful to have one contact person—a sponsor—with whom the team leader communicates and from whom the leader may seek assistance as problems arise. Periodically, the sponsor could sit in on team members' discussions, providing feedback and helping with specific issues. Otherwise, a team leader will have to run interference through an unwieldy number of managers. So we recommend that the leader make sure he or she has a sponsor who will be a key contact between the cross-functional team and the manager of each selected team member.

Communication is key for all teams, but it becomes even more important for cross-functional teams. Members of such a team probably do not interact as much on a daily basis compared to team members within a work unit. That means there are probably fewer opportunities for them to see one another casually and talk about the project at hand. Bottom line: Virtual teaming is going to be the key to success. This certainly suggests the use of e-mail. However, e-mail is largely ineffective when three or more individuals are trying to carry out a virtual problem-solving or decision-making strategy. Here, virtual chat rooms and discussion boards should be the norm. For those leaders who are not familiar with these options in the work environment, chat rooms allow synchronous communication among team members at designated times (e.g., Thursday morning from 9:00 A.M. to 10:00 A.M. CDT), and discussion boards provide opportunities for individuals to communicate during a specified period of time but not at the same time (e.g., the team discusses an issue from August 21 to 29). Both of these vehicles, along with e-mail for more FYI purposes, are critical to keeping all members in the communication loop. Conference calls and video-conferences are also forms of virtual communication. (For more information, we suggest you review the chapter on virtual communication in *Fast Forward Leadership;* Essex and Kusy 1999, pp. 97–114.) Web-based meetings, which may add a visual element, are even more effective as a means of connecting online.

Following are some of the most pertinent questions we have found for these types of teams:

- How honest have our conversations been?

- What kinds of opportunities did we have for addressing our concerns (either virtually or face-to-face) about the process of the meeting or the tasks we are performing?

  - What mechanisms were in place to provide feedback either to the team or to individual members?

  - How effectively is each team member communicating with his or her boss regarding the group's progress and any support needed from the leader?

LINKING WORK-UNIT RESPONSIBILITIES WITH CROSS-FUNCTIONAL TEAM RESPONSIBILITIES

Finally, to really increase the probability of successful cross-functional teamwork, there needs to be a connection between the team member's "real" work, the day-to-day responsibilities, and his or her cross-functional responsibilities. Without this association, two things can go awry. Either the individual sees the work of the cross-functional team as his or her primary assignment or largely ignores the work with the cross-functional team and focuses on work-unit responsibilities. Here, the leader needs to coach the team member on the priority of both sets of responsibilities. Specifically, we suggest that the leader point out the connection between the collaborative cross-functional endeavor and the goals of the person's own work unit. This helps the team member regulate responsibilities and accountabilities across the boundaries of the organization.

Promoting Cross-Functional Teamwork

Virgil has designated one of his direct reports, Connie, to work on a cross-functional team composed of members from five units. This is a high-visibility team directly accountable to the president of the division. More important, the work of this team will have an impact on the entire enterprise, as the results will be used as a prototype for the rest of the organization. Virgil wants to make sure that Connie contributes significantly. However, he is also concerned that some of her current work will fall by the wayside because the cross-boundaries work is far more exciting than her day-to-day responsibilities. He wonders how he can help her manage both sets of expectations to the maximum extent possible.

Louellen Advises...

Virgil, you are asking the right question at the right time. Before Connie gets into a jam, enamored with the high-profile project assignment, sit down with her to discuss her workload and priorities. Review her development plan and determine how much of a career builder the project assignment will be and how important she thinks it is. Take a look at her current workload and identify tasks that she can put on hold or delegate to someone else. Negotiate with Connie on what portion of her time she might spend on the project and on her day-to-day work assignments. By discussing the potential problem up front, you will give Connie the support she needs to be successful in both arenas.

You might also want to consider how you will get information about Connie's performance on the project assignment. Make sure you speak with her periodically about her work, reviewing and discussing it. Additionally, if no process is in place, solicit feedback from the division president. I don't suggest this as a way to learn about problems but, more important for a high performer like Connie, as a way to give her the praise and recognition she deserves for her work with the project team.

Mitch Advises...

Virgil, you are in a pickle. Placing Connie on the cross-functional team raises the probability that some of her unit-related work will suffer. However, if she doesn't join the team, the organization won't benefit from her talent. In my view, any good leader needs to think beyond his or her own immediate scope of control. So if I were consulted about this project, I would help you understand the need for the larger organizational perspective. However, it's not an all-or-nothing approach. How, then, does any leader accommodate both sets of interests?

First, meet with the team sponsor and Connie together to get a rundown on the team's responsibilities and the amount of time the team project is likely to take. It is critical that Connie be part of this initial discussion because involvement generates greater commitment and better results.

Second, once both you and Connie are comfortable with the accountabilities expected, have Connie draft a contract delineating how she proposes to meet her unit-related responsibilities, including prioritizing and delegating her current work. I firmly believe that simply adding more responsibilities to an already heavy workload is not good management. You need to make room for the new behaviors to thrive.

Third, you and Connie should meet regularly to determine how she is meeting her work-unit expectations as well as the demands of the cross-functional team. The organizational sponsor should meet consistently with both of you. This doesn't need to be an elaborate face-to-face meeting; an e-mail conversation is fine. Here, the sponsor shares his or her feedback about Connie's performance with you, and Connie gives you her perspectives on her own performance with the cross-functional team.

During this three-way communication, it might be useful for Connie to provide feedback to the sponsor on the effectiveness of this individual's leadership as it relates to her performance in the organization. Remember, the cross-functional team is organizationally driven and is therefore building leadership capacity throughout the organization. Coaching is not only downward, but across and up. By engaging these three venues through a coaching modality, you'll be leading in the best possible way.

BUILDING COLLABORATION
ACROSS MULTIPLE WORK UNITS

Interteam development, or team building across multiple work units, is the third venue to consider. Based on our experiences, we would guess that, if you have participated in any kind of team development activity, it has been of the intrateam variety, in which members of a work-unit team build their internal capacity. While the level of teamwork required in this context may not be as intense as for others, it is important to attend to interteam dynamics. In our consulting with hundreds of teams, we have discovered that there are many similarities between interteam and intrateam development. Both require a clear sense of purpose and commitment, effective problem-solving and decision-making processes, and talent. However, the interteam development process accentuates a particular need—the need for coordination. This certainly should be present within a work unit and a cross-functional team, but the need is so much more pronounced across teams. Here are some of the key dimensions of interteam coordination:

- Defining the means of forging connections between teams
- Aligning the objectives of individual work units to form a base for collaboration on the overall project
- Establishing measures of success

In our own work, we have found that dealing with the first dimension, keeping the work units connected, is a perilous task because of the many competing demands that can come into play. The typical forms of communication we have outlined for the cross-functional team work in this context, but more may be needed. We have also found that it is helpful to select one individual from each work unit to serve as a key liaison. These liaisons need to meet regularly and make sure that there is appropriate coordination across units, with a focus on preventing the formation of roadblocks or potential snags along the way. By outlining work processes and areas of collaboration with other work units, each group can clarify its view of collaboration.

The second coordination function, aligning goals, is best done when work-unit leaders create their operational plans. They should meet to look for potentially conflicting initiatives that could inadvertently generate tension across work units.

The third dimension, determining measures of success, is another important element of collaboration. Leaders can do this in one of two ways: by involving all work-unit members in brainstorming the standards for success and then building consensus, or by creating or handing down the measures themselves. For example, the executive director of a nonprofit organization may stipulate her definition of success. Or the board of a large multinational corporation may determine the organization's measure of success in the next three years. What's important is that the success criteria be concrete and achievable, even if difficult.

SCENARIO

Promoting Interteam Development

Sam's hands are getting a little sweaty as he looks out at the production teams on the manufacturing floor of Specific Motors. Since he assumed the plant manager position three months ago, he has been keenly aware of the lack of teamwork within several of the so-called manufacturing teams. They are supposed to function as collaborative groups in designing, building, marketing, and selling specialized pickups, but in reality, some of them are working independently, with team members simply passing off their work to the next person in the process. The upshot has been a multitude of inefficiencies, due mostly to lack of understanding of different roles within the teams and the absence of a coordinated process for collaboration. The resulting errors have cost the company dearly, and Sam is under the gun to improve the performance of the teams.

Mitch Advises...

OK, Sam, you are a victim of something that is easily fixed. Please review the key dimensions of interteam coordination outlined on page 53. While all three dimensions are relevant, the one that hits me between the eyes addresses aligning each work unit's goals with the larger project. The bottom line, in my view, is that each unit does not truly understand how its goals contribute to this large assignment. It appears to me that the teams (and maybe even the team members) may see themselves as cogs in a wheel but without any purpose. They really don't understand how their own performance fits into the larger organizational purview of the interteam project. This sense of alignment needs to be built ASAP.

I would accomplish this by first letting each team know what the expectations are. Common sense may tell you that this is a given. In my experience, though, I have found that it sometimes is not! Second, I suggest that you give each team an assignment, asking its members to identify the ways in which their team can fulfill this expectation. Third, I recommend that you set up a venue that permits every team to share ways of fulfilling the overall project expectations. Then each team should take the opportunity to listen to feedback from the other teams on these expectations—the positives and the negatives. Finally, each team needs to come up with a plan for improving its chances of meeting the expectations, communicate this plan to the other teams, and change course as needed.

Louellen Advises...

I'm reminded of my client, a creative group in a marketing company, that had a similar problem with project teams. Managers used the analogy of work being tossed "over the wall" from one department to the next, resulting in a fair amount of chaos and cost to the firm. As a way of drawing the teams' attention to the problem, the managers created a humorous skit, wherein each manager stood next to a partition, acted out the work of his or her area and the derogatory talk within the units, and then threw work over the partition to the next manager. The skit was entertaining, made the point, and stimulated lively discussion and action to improve the collaborative process within the firm.

Sam, I think you should consider doing something similar. You're a new manager, which means you have the opportunity to share your observations as an unbiased near outsider. If humor is not your shtick, then specific examples of what you have noted may be enough to stimulate change. Another approach would be to have someone—an outside consultant or HR person—interview members of the teams and collect their views on the efficacy of their groups. The analysis of these data may grab the attention of team members.

Next, I'd advise a team-building event that begins with an educative piece on the characteristics of high-performing cross-functional teams and the types of processes they use. Then, Sam, the teams can review their modus operandi against these best practices and begin to engage in creating new, more effective ways of collaborating. Consider having the group develop a flowchart showing how the process would work if everyone stayed involved, at some level, from design to sales. It is important that you not dictate the solution but rather let the teams develop their own once they see the problems at hand.

In stimulating discussion on how a set of teams can best work together, I have used four questions that you may want to incorporate into your team-building agenda. Ask each team to meet separately and answer the following questions about the other teams:

- What do the other teams do that we appreciate, value, find helpful? (Generate a separate list of answers for each team.)

- What does each team do that creates a barrier to our working effectively?

- What would we like each team to do differently to improve our collaboration?

- What do we predict the other teams will say about us?

The fourth question takes the edge off the feedback inherent in this design. In predicting what the others will say, most groups will own up to their contributions to the problem!

FACILITATING A TEAM-BUILDING RETREAT

Too often, leaders haphazardly put together retreat agendas that revolve around a series of presentations on business development from senior leaders or briefing reports from team members. This approach is almost guaranteed to put participants to sleep! The goals of a well-orchestrated team-building retreat should be to develop or maintain relationships, review or create a team-generated vision, refocus on desired outcomes, remove barriers to collaboration, and/or reward and recognize the team's accomplishments. To these ends, the leader must design each agenda item to include an interesting process or method that sparks interest and provides variety.

Most team-building retreats focus on continuing to improve the group's effectiveness. Prepare for the retreat by reviewing the team's progress on current work as well as its processes—that is, how well individuals work together to get the work done. Think about barriers to productivity and how best to address them with the group.

Assemble any relevant information you would like to present or have participants read them ahead of time. Then develop the agenda using the following format:

- Opening
- Relationship-building activity
- Review of team successes
- Issue identification and problem solving
- Action planning
- Follow-up

We'll explain each of these items to help you plan a successful team development retreat.

OPENING

Begin by reviewing the retreat goals and giving your team a warm welcome. Focus on the outcomes you expect from the time you are spending together.

RELATIONSHIP-BUILDING ACTIVITY

This element of your design should set the tone by sparking interest and putting participants at ease. You could use icebreakers such as asking participants to share something about themselves—vacation plans, favorite activities, or hobbies. Or you might have team members complete a personality assessment, such as the *Myers-Briggs Type Indicator®* instrument, and discuss individual approaches to work and their implications for the group's dynamics. You could also include a team-building activity that requires small groups to solve a problem or develop a response to a case scenario that presents a problem related to the group's real work. *Team Games for Trainers* by Carolyn Nilson (1993) and *Team-Building Activities for Every Group* by Alanna Jones (1999) are good resources for planning this kind of activity. Keep in mind that the purpose of the activity is to help team members understand one another more fully and improve working relationships on the job and at the retreat.

REVIEW OF TEAM SUCCESSES

Make sure you express your approval of the great work the team has done to date. Unfortunately, team-building activities often have negative connotations in organizations, in that people feel there must be something wrong if they must engage in team building at all. Make sure the team understands that you want to use this retreat to propel them to new heights and capitalize on their great work.

ISSUE IDENTIFICATION AND PROBLEM SOLVING

In this step, you invite the team to assess its performance. Find out what barriers to collaboration they are experiencing and work with them to create solutions. This should be a time to talk, not *at* participants but *with* them. Here are some methods to consider:

Activity 1: Real vs. Ideal

Separate team members into groups of two to five and ask each small group to draw a picture of how the team functions now and how it should function ideally. After the small groups present their drawings, ask either the full group or the small groups to develop solutions to the barriers that hold them back from achieving the ideal.

Activity 2: Barriers to Team Effectiveness

Have team members break into small groups and ask them to generate two or three questions about barriers to team effectiveness and changes

that could be made to overcome them. Then ask each group to designate an interviewer who will rotate to the other groups at ten- to fifteen-
minute intervals, asking the questions and recording the answers on a
notepad or laptop. When the interviewers complete the rotation and
return to their own small groups, direct them to summarize the findings and report back to the full group. Facilitate a discussion and selection of the best strategies.

Activity 3: Prioritizing Work

On a large flipchart, draw the matrix shown in Figure 6. You saw a similar matrix in Chapter 1 (Figure 2). In Figure 6, we replaced the amount
of resources needed with a satisfaction scale. We hope this gives you an
idea of how adaptable this matrix is. In this context, we suggest you
review the proposed solutions from either or both of the preceding
activities and ask each individual to place a Post-It on the matrix indicating the priority for each solution (one solution per Post-It). If there are
four solutions, there should be four different colors of Post-Its. Have
group members discuss their perspectives, making sure that each person's views are heard. Choose those solutions that are in the low satisfaction, high impact area (shaded).

FIGURE 6. Prioritization Process Matrix—
Satisfaction × Impact

	Low Satisfaction	Medium Satisfaction	High Satisfaction
High Impact			
Medium Impact			
Low Impact			

ACTION PLANNING

Ask group members to delineate the steps they must take, and set dates for completion, in order to implement the solutions created in the problem-solving exercise. Then assign an individual or a subgroup to each action step.

FOLLOW-UP

Decide on a process for monitoring the action plan and set dates for the group to meet again and check progress.

It is important that team members leave the retreat feeling that the event was productive and that something will happen as a result of their efforts. Never drop the ball after a team-building event. The consequences could be dire in that cynicism most likely will set in and taint the team's enthusiasm for more team development activities. The outcome should be inspiring and stimulating, motivating each team member to be more of a contributor and help the team succeed.

SCENARIO

Facilitating a Team-Building Retreat

Lin, a manager for client services for an investment firm, sits in his office thinking about the great team he has assembled over the past two-year period. Extremely customer-focused and collaborative, team members have developed superb client relationships worldwide. In fact, they have held on to 95 percent of them, in spite of fierce competition from other firms. Lin knows that team maintenance, no matter how effective a team may be, is important to sustain the collaborative spirit and keep team members focused on collective outcomes. He wonders how he might put together an exciting, yet productive, retreat.

Mitch Advises...

Kudos to you, Lin, for not resting on your laurels and basking in your team's success. You've done an outstanding job. As you know, work demands are increasing, and you are being asked to do more in a leaner environment. Thus, you have zeroed in on a key variable here—considering how a team retreat can complement the team's already superior work as well as set the stage for their next challenge. I would begin designing the team retreat around the latter area, future challenges. Because you have a high-performing team, and it's key to engage such teams from the start, I suggest that you ask for three or four volunteers to help you craft this retreat.

After reviewing the sample team development retreat agenda on page 57, I recommend that the design group add one other element— strategic focus. For this activity, ask team members to brainstorm the challenges they are likely to face in the next three-year period. Then have them whittle these down to a manageable number, using a consensus process. Once they have identified these challenges, set up a flipchart in the following way:

Challenge 1:

1. How will my solo work need to change to address this challenge?

2. What kind of support might I need from the team for this solo work?

3. How will teamwork need to change to address this challenge?

Repeat this for all the challenges and have the team discuss each one. Since they are high performers, you probably won't need to structure this exercise much, except to determine the time needed to allow everyone an opportunity to be heard. Finally, have team members discuss what kind of follow-up process they would like to see.

Louellen Advises...

How about making the team retreat a celebration of the group's accomplishments? Prepare a review of the goals team members set and the metrics they met. Ask team members to talk individually about their biggest "hits" for the year. Invite an upper manager or two to add words of praise. Consider developing an inspiring video highlighting staff interacting with clients and featuring interviews that focus on their strategies for success. Create a reward to give to each team member— something that says, in essence, "outstanding work." Then spend some time setting new performance targets for the upcoming year. Keep a high-energy tone to the retreat, with the goal being for team members to leave feeling successful and eager to move on to even higher performance.

The team development literature pays much attention to the management of teams that are in a tough spot. I think your attentiveness to maintaining the high-performing team demonstrates that you are not a leader who focuses only on what's wrong. It's easy for a group that has accomplished a lot to get a little lazy and experience a performance lull. By conducting this retreat, you will keep your group revved up and ready to move on to the next level.

CHAPTER 3

Managing Performance Issues

IF WE HAD TO CHOOSE THE ONE CATEGORY of problems we see most frequently in our consulting practices, it would be performance management issues—concerns about staff members who are not doing what they are expected to do. We have often wondered why managers struggle so much with employees who create problems. After all, isn't the manager in charge and capable of just telling these staff members to shape up or ship out? Obviously, the solutions are not quite that easy. Managers themselves are often conflict-avoidant and end up taking a wait-and-see approach, hoping the situation gets better. Typically, it doesn't. Sometimes managers become overwhelmed by the documentation required to record their responses to problem situations and just can't find the time to follow up adequately. Whatever the reason, the outcome is the same: critical performance issues are often dealt with poorly or at least are not addressed with the appropriate rigor and promptness.

FIGURE 7. Flowchart for Assessing the Cause of a
Performance Problem and How to Solve It

Questions to Ask	Responses	Solutions
1. Have you set clear and concrete expectations?	NO	Set expectations for the required behavior or performance.
If **YES,** go to question 2		
2. Have you communicated these expectations to the employee?	NO	Communicate these expectations.
If **YES,** go to question 3		
3. Does the employee clearly understand that his or her behavior or performance is a problem?	NO	Communicate specific behavioral feedback.
If **YES,** go to question 4		
4. Does the employee know how to do what you are expecting?	NO	Provide training and coaching.
If **YES,** go to question 5		
5. Is something interfering with the employee's ability to do the job?	YES	Remove the obstacle or at least run interference for the employee.
If **NO,** go to question 6		
6. Is nonperformance rewarded and performance punished?	YES	Change the consequences.
If **NO,** go to question 7		
7. If the employee wanted to, could he or she behave or perform as expected?	NO	Reassign, transfer, or terminate the employee.

ASSESSING PERFORMANCE PROBLEMS

We have observed that many managers, once they do decide to tackle a performance issue, take a haphazard approach. As with any problem-solving process, it is important to begin with identifying the problem and not leap too quickly to a solution. Careful analysis of the reasons for a performance problem is the first step to an effective fix, so we begin with a step-by-step process for assessing performance problems. The flowchart in Figure 7, adapted from the work of Fournies (1987), provides a guide for diagnosis.

We have deliberately selected this model because it is an eye-opener. Many leaders assume, erroneously we might add, that they have done all the right things to manage performance. This model serves as a reminder that good performance management is concrete and behaviorally specific. As consultants, we have found the model particularly successful with our own organizational clients who see two primary purposes here—as a model for reactive corrective action and as a cue for proactively initiating performance management the right way.

SET EXPECTATIONS

The flowchart begins with setting clear and concrete expectations. This may be one of the simplest tasks, and so it is easily overlooked. To set expectations, we would like to review the SMART model (see Figure 8), which many effective managers use.

FIGURE 8. The SMART Way to Set Expectations

Criterion	Defining Question
S pecific	Exactly what do we want to do?
M easurable	How will we know we have done it?
A chievable	Is it realistic, given our resources?
R esults oriented	Will it add value?
T ime specific	By when should we achieve it?

As you work through the model, make sure the expectation is behaviorally *specific,* grounded in actions that can be described in concrete ways, such that independent observers who are familiar with the task would know achievement when they see it. Second, the expectation must be *measurable.* We certainly understand that many performance expectations may be difficult to measure. To this end, we challenge you to be persistent here. Let's consider an expectation that is a bit "soft"— such as being an effective team player. If the leader breaks this down into manageable chunks, it is quite easy to view it as something measurable. We suggest the following potential breakdown of expectations:

- Provide feedback to the team in a respectful manner
- Listen during meetings without also doing other work
- Follow up on the team's requests

Next, make sure that the expectation is *achievable.* You would not want to present any individual with an expectation that is literally impossible to achieve. Next, the expectation should be *results oriented* in that it connects with the real work of the team or organization. For example, if the expectation is to follow up on requests made by the team, then the result may be that the team completes the project on time, on budget, and in alignment with the strategic goals of the organization—leading to project effectiveness. And finally, the expectation needs to be *time specific.* The leader, the team, and/or the employee could determine the time parameter. If the timeline for meeting the expectation is not made explicit, it would be easy for the staff member to let things slide, feeling no pressure to take action.

COMMUNICATE EXPECTATIONS

Question 2 in the flowchart asks whether the leader has communicated expectations to the employee. Setting expectations is one thing; communicating them is another. Consider this simple test. If we were to ask an employee with whom you are experiencing performance problems whether he or she knows what is expected, how do you think that individual would respond? We suggest using the following scale:

> 5 = Definitely knows what is expected
> 4 = Somewhat sure
> 3 = Not quite sure
> 2 = Unsure
> 1 = No clues as to what is expected

We use this scale because there are gradations in performance problem behavior. It is not absolute, and a yes-or-no response doesn't get at the heart of the issue. As a leader, you need to tease out these nuances and increase the probability that you're communicating expectations with finesse.

ENSURE UNDERSTANDING

The third step in the model is about helping the employee understand that his or her behavior or performance is a problem. In our experience, managers often think they have given feedback, but when we question them about what they said, we find they have not been clear. For example, "I am concerned about your communication" is not a clear statement. There are many forms of communication. So make sure you describe the problem in specific terms. Use descriptors that can be seen and measured, such as spotty attendance, negative comments, incomplete assignments, or lack of contribution to team discussions. In our second book, *Breaking the Code of Silence: Prominent Leaders Reveal How They Rebounded from Seven Critical Mistakes* (Kusy and Essex 2005), we present the following template for giving performance feedback:

1. Describe the problem as you have observed it.

   - Don't infer.

   - Don't use sarcasm.

   - Don't use absolute terms (e.g., "never," "always," "constantly").

   - Avoid judgmental terms.

2. Explain why you perceive this as a problem.

3. Pause; give the individual an opportunity to share his or her views.

4. Get agreement that there is a problem.

5. Brainstorm alternatives for solving the problem.

6. Agree on one alternative.

7. Outline the next steps.

8. Follow up.

As you can see, these steps require careful and precise communication about the issue, the impact of the problem, and agreement on a solution.

HELP THE EMPLOYEE MEET EXPECTATIONS

If you believe you have given specific feedback that meets the criteria we've described, you may proceed to question 4 in the flowchart. Is it possible that the employee, while understanding and agreeing to the expectations you have set and the feedback you have given, doesn't know how to perform the tasks at hand? Sometimes staff members agree, for example, that they need to meet deadlines but have no clue as to how to organize their workloads and manage their time. Consider linking an employee in this situation to training resources or coaching. Training can be as formal as sending the individual to an off-site program. Or it can be as informal as on-the-job training conducted by either you or the employee's colleagues. Coaching, likewise, may be formal or informal. Formal coaching would entail involvement with a coaching professional with expertise in the area of concern. Informal coaching could be provided by you or a colleague who not only has the content expertise but has some good adult-instruction skills. Whatever the format—training or coaching—be sure to take time to evaluate how effectively the new performance meets the expectations set.

LOOK FOR OBSTACLES

If training is not the issue, move on to question 5 and investigate the possibility that obstacles may be having a negative effect on the staff member's performance. There are two types of obstacles: those within the work environment and those within the employee. In trying to identify an external problem, you might ask whether something in the work environment makes it difficult for the staff member to perform properly. For example, is the equipment faulty, or does another employee, who supplies work to the "underperforming" person, fail to meet deadlines or quality standards? The second type of obstacle could be a personal problem, such as an illness or chemical dependency, that prevents the person from performing effectively. Typically, the employee in question has not shared his or her personal situation with the manager, so it is important to ask, "Is everything OK with you? Is there anything I should know that would help me understand why you are having this problem?" Never accuse the staff member of anything. And avoid becoming the diagnostician. For example, it is not within a manager's purview to state that a person has a chemical dependency problem. Rather, the manager needs to let the individual know what he or she has observed. It might be something like the employee showing up late for meetings three times during the past week, or becoming angry and raising his voice inappropriately at several recent meetings, or having alcohol on his breath at two important client meetings. These are observable behaviors. All the leader can do is state the observable, not act as a diagnostic psychologist.

BE AWARE OF REWARDS AND PUNISHMENTS

If you are convinced that there are no obstacles, consider question 6, which relates to motivation. Are the contingencies properly aligned? Sometimes it appears more advantageous to a problem staff member to continue the behavior that creates disruption. For example, if missing deadlines allows an employee to be laissez-faire and comfortable because there is no perceived consequence, it may be more appealing to the empoyee to maintain the behavior than to change it. Or if a high-performing person is punished for doing a job well, he or she may not repeat the performance. We often see this dynamic when a manager overloads the best staff members with assignments, knowing they will get the job done in an outstanding way. The side effect, however, is burned-out performers who slack off after seeing their coworkers get by with doing less work. Or worse yet, these high performers may leave the organization!

EVALUATE THE EMPLOYEE'S CAPABILITY

If none of the above sections seems to fit your situation, go on to question 7. Is it possible that no matter what you do, the employee just can't do the job, even though he or she seems motivated? Sometimes an individual has the interest but not the ability. If the job is a poor match for a person's talents, the performance issue is unlikely ever to be solved. You are better off reassigning the staff member to work that is a better fit or terminating him or her.

DEALING WITH STAFF MEMBERS WHO DON'T CARRY THEIR WEIGHT

Given the predominance of team structures in today's organizations, as described in Chapter 2, staff members who are not carrying their share of the workload become a critical issue. In surveys of teams, this behavior is often the one that respondents dislike most in their colleagues. It is disheartening for team members to work hard with the others and then have a weak team member receive credit for work he or she did not do. And the added responsibility of taking up a laggard's workload is a deadening burden for conscientious staff members who want to perform and feel obligated to make sure the work gets done.

While any of the flowchart items in Figure 7 may apply in this situation, we often find that the cause of this problem is addressed in question 6. It becomes rewarding for the offender not to do his or her work when others will pick up the slack. So the person who does not pull his or her weight benefits from the lighter workload if there are no consequences for the behavior. Two dynamics come into play here. First, the other team members are enabling the problem by doing the work of the less productive employee. Second, the manager is not employing consequences. The problem must be approached on these two fronts.

The manager should assess the workload of each team member, making sure to develop a clear understanding of who is doing what. This may require walking the floor, so to speak, to see the team in action. Then the manager should ask those who are assuming added responsibilities to stop doing so and allow the natural consequences of the problem employee's inaction to occur, provided this does not harm the business. At the same time, the leader must engage the employee with specific behavior feedback, indicating what will happen if the work is not done.

As consultants, we are often asked what consequences a manager could impose, short of filing a formal grievance or placing a letter in the individual's personnel file. Our suggestions include pulling a team member off the group project, asking the person to complete additional assignments as compensation for burdening others, or creating some degree of discomfort by coaching the person's coworkers to give him or her direct feedback on the stress caused by the additional work.

SCENARIO

Dealing with a Staff Member
Who Doesn't Carry His Weight

Martin is a manager of accounting for a large supermarket chain. The majority of his staff are hardworking and skilled, except for Phil, a longtime employee whom Martin inherited when he took the job three years ago. Phil has learned, it appears to Martin, how to play the system. He takes every bit of sick time and vacation allowed and has managed to get approval from human resources for several short-term leaves of absence for personal, health-related reasons. Phil often comes to the office in the morning ten to fifteen minutes after his start time and rarely stays past the end of the workday. Martin has always been flexible with his staff about start times, so he has not said anything to Phil. The other staff members are frustrated because they have to cover for Phil so frequently. Phil does good work; he just doesn't do enough of it. Martin needs a solution to this problem.

Louellen Advises...

Two possibilities come to mind here, Martin. First, Phil may be playing the system as you suspect, finding ways to manipulate policies so he can take off as much time as possible. Or he may have a legitimate health problem. To tackle the issue, meet with your human resources partner and lay out all you know collectively about the situation along with the options policies will permit. If Phil is unable to fulfill the obligations of the job because of his absences, you most likely will be able to offer him a long-term leave to improve his health status or terminate him if you can substantiate that the quantity of work he performs does not meet minimum standards.

Keep in mind, Martin, that it is not fair to your other staff members to put them in the position of doing extra work so frequently because of Phil. Move quickly to rectify this situation before you lose some of your valued hardworking employees.

Mitch Advises...

This is a difficult situation, but there is one thing you can do before anything else. Get help from a human resources professional or attorney within your organization. It sounds like your company is large enough to support one. If not, then find an independent professional who specializes in this area. If Phil has legitimate health-related concerns, you'll need to provide conditions that support him. If his health concerns mean he cannot handle his responsibilities, then these experts are the best individuals to advise you.

Taking time off is one thing. Coming to the office late is another. Since Phil has not said that his tardiness is related to his illness, hold him accountable for coming to work on time. Tell him this is your expectation and provide consequences when he does not. Follow the guidelines for good performance management we have outlined in this chapter. And if Phil's tardiness is health related, you will have done the right thing by consulting a human resources or legal expert.

MANAGING STAFF MEMBERS WHO PERFORM BELOW ESTABLISHED STANDARDS

Some managers liken this problem to the first one we addressed in this chapter—dealing with staff members who don't carry their weight. While there certainly are some similarities, the difference is primarily one of perspective. In the first instance (not carrying one's weight), the context is the individual in relationship to the team. In the second (performing below established standards), it is the employee in relationship to his or her own accountabilities.

In order to solve this dilemma, we suggest reviewing the flowchart in Figure 7, determining which items are most likely to be an issue, and then moving through the process accordingly. In general, we have found that solutions to questions 1 and 2 contribute the most to solving this problem—setting and communicating clear expectations. To our amazement, many leaders who really believe they have set concrete goals and communicated them in a clear-cut way have done just the opposite. We have discovered the actual situation by asking very simple, probing questions such as:

- What are the top behaviors associated with the expectation?

- What would the final performance look like if the expectation were met?

- How often have you communicated the expectation in exactly the same way?

- What are some of the different formats you used to communicate the expectation, taking into consideration different learning styles?

As you can see from these questions, we're helping the leader hone the skills of setting and communicating expectations. We have also suggested to some clients that they communicate this expectation to a trusted colleague, in a mock discussion, before talking with the problem performer, just to see if they are communicating with precision. Surprisingly, leaders often find that they only *thought* they were communicating accurately and clearly!

SCENARIO

Managing a Staff Member
Who Works Below Established Standards

Maria is a seasoned leader, a principal at an architectural firm, where she is accustomed to managing a cast of superstars. She has worked hard and built a track record of success, first as an architect and now as leader of the arts and culture area of her firm. Her group has designed and built award-

winning buildings all over the country, each person doing whatever it takes to get the firm's high-quality work out the door.

Six months ago, Maria brought a new architect into her group. Cathy, a recent graduate of an internationally recognized architecture program, is young, energetic, and eager to move her career along through the firm's established development process. However, her work is below the quality Maria had expected. Maria has given Cathy feedback on her designs and drawings, but Cathy's performance has not substantially improved. Part of the problem seems to be that Cathy has her own way of doing things, which she developed in her academic program but is different from the firm's approach. Maria's time for coaching is limited, and the other staff members in her group are swamped with projects. Maria wonders if she has made a big mistake hiring Cathy. Should she try to work with Cathy, or cut her losses and let Cathy go?

Louellen Advises...

Maria, I have some questions for you that might help you decide whether or not to retain Cathy. First, even though her work does not follow your firm's prescribed process, is it of good quality? Second, do you believe that Cathy has been given the degree of coaching that she as well as any young architect would need in order to understand the work standards specific to your firm? In other words, are the expectations really clear? Third, do you think she has the ability to respond to feedback and make the needed changes? Is she coachable? If you answered yes to all these questions, then you may be able to retain her by reining her in a little bit tighter.

Consider assigning a senior, skilled architect to be her mentor and coach. Have Cathy shadow that person and learn how the firm's standards are applied on projects. Ask Cathy to let the mentor review her work and provide guidance every step of the way. Check in regularly with the mentor to see if Cathy is improving adequately. Explain to her that you want her to succeed and are giving her the opportunity to learn more fully the skills she will need to accelerate her career path in the firm. Be clear with her, however, that she has to conform to the expected work standards and that her mentor will help her see what this entails.

Beware of a potential trap in this approach. If Cathy shows a little bit of progress, it will be tempting to accept that as a sign that she is going to get even better. In this case you are looking for a *substantial* amount of improvement—enough that she will be capable of working independently after approximately three months of steady work with a mentor. If she doesn't skyrocket, consider consulting your human resources staff about letting her go before she becomes a permanent problem. I can't emphasize enough that you should not let the problem linger so long that terminating Cathy becomes difficult, due to human resources policy and legal ramifications. Make the tough choice, if you have to.

Mitch Advises...

Maria, you have hired someone who is going to need a great deal of coaching primarily because she is so fresh out of school. The academic world of architecture is far different from the reality of a business that thrives on providing the most value for its customers with efficiencies and economies of scale whenever feasible. So take her under your wing and help her grow, step by step.

My first suggestion, then, is that *you*, Maria, need to do an about-face in your expectations of this newcomer to the world of work. Once you have accepted that your role may need to change, then you're ready to proceed to what I call phase two of the career development process—making sure expectations are set and clear.

To do this, first run through the expectations yourself. I recommend considering the SMART model we highlighted in Figure 8. Then go through this model with Cathy. She may need a fair amount of direction from you in this regard, so don't be afraid to provide it—not in an offensive way, but firmly explaining how she might create greater value for the firm. Of course, listen to her views along the way. You may learn some things that will surprise you. For example, don't be alarmed if you hear her say that she has been trying to talk with you about these very areas of concern, but you have been either unavailable or very short with her when she's sought you out. Remember what *you* were like when you were a recent architecture grad!

If it looks like you may be getting through to her, in that she wants to change her behavior, set up weekly appointments when the two of you can review her performance on selected projects—again, using the SMART model as a backdrop. Also, don't feel that you must be her only mentor. Ask her if she has developed closeness with others in the firm. If she has, select one of these individuals and bring him or her in on these discussions. That way, you'll be developing not only Cathy but also the leadership capacity of the person you designate as a coach. Sort of a two-for-one deal.

Pursue this strategy for several months. If there is no significant improvement, then you may have made the wrong hire. This would be unfortunate, but it's far more unfortunate to string along someone who is probably destined to fail. You'll need to work with your human resources professional to begin the termination process. But let's not get into this just yet. I have a sense that with some of this careful coaching, Cathy is going to turn out to be another one of your great hires!

DEALING WITH STAFF MEMBERS WHO WORK POORLY WITH OTHERS

While reviewing the flowchart in Figure 7, we found that two items are most pronounced in dealing with staff members who work poorly with others—question 3 ("Does the employee clearly understand that his or her behavior or performance is a problem?") and question 6 ("Is non-performance rewarded and performance punished?").

Providing feedback is one of a manager's most difficult responsibilities, and it is sometimes more difficult between colleagues. Yet this is a critical component in such a situation. And as you can see, feedback needs to be supplied from one or both of the following parties: the manager and the colleague. Let's tackle the manager first. When giving feedback, it's important to keep in mind that the employee may not even be aware that his or her behavior is a problem. So we caution the leader to be gentle at first. Don't overload the individual with negative feedback that is likely to produce defensiveness. Instead, take a look at the template for providing performance feedback on pages 67–68.

It also is important for the leader to coach the problem performer's team members on providing feedback directly to him or her. Don't get caught in the trap of taking over and giving the employee feedback that should be coming from colleagues. Remember, you not only are dealing with this one behavior but are also preparing leaders—and what better way to prepare them than to help colleagues understand the value of good performance feedback?

We have often found that staff members who work poorly with others need assistance in building better interpersonal skills. Don't drop the ball after giving feedback. Make sure you provide individual coaching, which entails observation of the employee beforehand and then coaching. Seminars that incorporate skill practice may also be valuable in accelerating the learning process.

SCENARIO

Dealing with a Staff Member
Who Works Poorly with Others

Jonathan, a front desk staff person in the cardiac unit of a regional medical center, is creating enormous stress for his coworkers. Anne has recently been hired as the administrator of the work area, and Jonathan's two key colleagues have made their way to her office to complain. They cite example after example of Jonathan's territorial behaviors, specifically establishing rigid work routines and being unwilling to collaborate with others. It appears that Jonathan works in isolation, with little regard for what his coworkers might want to do. He is introverted, highly organized, and very hardworking. He presents an air of self-righteousness and looks down on others, as if he thinks they are less competent than he is. Anne's dilemma is that Jonathan is extremely efficient and gets more work done in a day than his coworkers do. Additionally, she has received no complaints about him from patients as they arrive to check in for appointments. The key issue is his relationship with coworkers. Anne wonders what her best approach to the situation would be.

Mitch Advises...

The first order of business, Anne, is to do some legwork yourself. How is it that Jonathan is a problem despite being the most efficient member of your staff? Could it be *their* problem, not his? I'm certainly not saying that it is, but that is a possibility. One interesting result I have found in my own consulting practice is that others sometimes feel "punished" when someone performs as expected. So just be sure you have done an adequate job of finding out what is really going on here.

During this process, I suggest you separate perceived attitudes from actual behaviors. For example, I would not accept any staff feedback that a person is "self-righteous" and "looks down" on them. These are attitudes; they are neither measurable nor appropriate for action. I would push for the specific behaviors associated with these attitudes. If Jonathan's coworkers can't come up with any, it could be their problem, not his. However, let's say that you do discover some specific behaviors associated with these attitudes. You might hear things like, "When I go to Jonathan with a question, he says he's too busy. And when I ask him when he might be available, he retorts, 'I'm not your supervisor. Go ask Anne.'" Now you have an indication that it might be a problem either with Jonathan's performance or with team development. If it's the former, set behaviorally specific expectations for him. Be sure to say how becoming more of a team player will help him be even more successful as well as make his life a little easier. For example, you could coach him on working with team members who come to him with questions, explaining that if he responds in a timely manner, he might have fewer interruptions in the future or at least less work to do because he's making up for a team member's inadequate performance.

Finally, if the problems persist, I suggest you consider facilitating a team development retreat, as outlined in Chapter 2. If underlying issues are eroding the team's performance, your job is to get them out in the open. If you are uncomfortable with this type of process, you may need the assistance of a consultant whose expertise is performance management in teams. The good news is that by going through the process I've outlined here and attempting the selected intervention, you'll be all the more prepared should you decide to use the services of a consultant.

Louellen Advises...

This is a performance issue I see fairly often in my consulting practice, Anne: the "technically" competent person who has not developed the interpersonal skills needed to be an effective team player. The question you need to explore is this: How did Jonathan get the idea that he could do his job adequately without collaborating with others? I bet you'll find that he has been given above-average ratings on his performance reviews over his tenure in the organization. In other words, his lack of collaboration has not been viewed as a performance problem. Perhaps he has received feedback, but no action was taken beyond that. So Jonathan is not fully aware that his behavior is a problem.

I would begin by observing Jonathan's interactions with his coworkers and collecting your own examples. Feedback based on others' observations is never as strong as feedback based on your own personal observations. Schedule at least an hour with Jonathan to signal that the conversation you are about to have is significant. Let him know that you recognize and value his work ethic and performance of key job duties. Then state clearly that there is one area in which he is not working up to expectations: collaboration with his peers. Review the examples and get his perspective. Then move to a coaching role and talk through how he might have handled each of the situations cited in the examples if he were behaving as a team player. Make sure Jonathan understands exactly what he could be doing differently. Give him one or two specific suggestions for collaborating more effectively and then schedule a follow-up meeting within a week to see what he has attempted and what the results have been.

This approach assumes that Jonathan's job description includes the expectation that he work within a team environment. If not, it will be important to first clarify this expectation with all team members and make sure the appraisal process includes review of a person's ability to work well with others.

Additionally, I would advise you, Anne, to look for a team skills workshop the whole team could attend together. While it might be uncomfortable for Jonathan to do the team exercises the workshop is likely to require, it would be a good way to break the ice and allow you to facilitate some discussion with your group within the context of the learning environment.

MANAGING THE PERFORMANCE
OF ORGANIZATIONAL STARS

OK, we can probably guess what you may be thinking: these folks don't need performance management . . . they're independent go-getters who are quite successful. Maybe so, but our experiences as well as significant organizational research demonstrate the opposite. Stars *do* need good performance management from their leaders.

Consider the research of Buckingham and Coffman (1999), who found that the best leaders spend the most time with their best talent, people we refer to here as "organizational stars." To help get you in the right frame of reference, consider this question: Do you spend more time with your poor performers or your best performers? Surprisingly, most managers spend the greatest amount of their working time with those they regard as problem employees. We empathize with how difficult poor performers must be and understand that leaders believe they need to spend time with them, but we want to present an alternative model. Essentially, we recommend reversing the time perspectives; take more time with the best talent. If you don't believe us or the research, we suggest that you go to your organizational stars and ask them this question: "Do I spend enough time with you?" Many of our clients who have done this report that they often receive a flat-out "No!" Please note that we are not suggesting giving up on poor performers because, as we have discussed in this chapter, they need good performance management—to a point. We are suggesting that you ask your self-motivated talent what kind of leadership they need from you. Perhaps they need more organizational resources. Or coaching on a particular team issue they are facing. Or they might need you to free up their time for a short period by assigning a lower-priority project to other individuals. The point here is that leaders should not assume that these organizational stars can be left alone all the time—delegation does not equal abdication.

In addition, even organizational stars may demonstrate poor performance on a particular project. When this happens, leaders may tend to overlook the poor performance because these staff members have been such stars in other venues. We suggest you not succumb to this

FIGURE 9. The BRIDGE Model to Star Performance

Brainstorm collaboratively and reinforce previous stellar performance.

Review new discoveries they have recently made.

Incorporate these new discoveries and expectations into revised three- to six-month goals.

Determine the potential partnerships needed.

Give your word that you will run interference for them, if needed.

Evaluate and reinforce.

attitude, because ignoring their need is not going to help them. Remember, these performers should receive the kind of careful coaching and mentoring that any poor performer would get.

Interference is one of the most common reasons for the poor performance of organizational stars (question 5 in Figure 7). The best strategy here is to either remove the obstacle or help clear the way. However, because these individuals are such high performers, you may wish to engage them in a discussion as to how they would like you to be involved in the situation. For example, they may simply need some coaching on how to handle the problem themselves. Or they may want to meet with you and an individual causing difficulty so that they can voice their concerns directly, with you simply providing support.

We have also discovered that this group may not respond as positively to the performance feedback template outlined on pages 67–68, which is meant to address a performance problem. Organizational stars typically don't have performance problems (except in the case of interference, as discussed). So for all other contexts in which you wish to enhance their performance further, we suggest relying on the BRIDGE model in Figure 9.

In reviewing the BRIDGE model, you'll see that the first major difference between this and the feedback template for correcting for poor performance is that you are brainstorming to reinforce the superb performance of these stars (not trying to determine the problem). The process is quite collaborative, except that you direct the brainstorming toward one topic—their stellar performance. We placed this first in the model because organizational stars often tell us that they wish they heard a bit more about the good work they are doing on the job. In addition, during this collaborative phase, you also reinforce their performance in meeting or exceeding previous expectations.

Second, because these individuals typically go way beyond the call of duty, you'll want to review new discoveries they have made. You may or may not be aware of these discoveries, so take time and let them "sound off" about their accomplishments.

Next, incorporate what you have learned in steps 1 and 2 of the model and develop a new set of three- to six-month expectations (some leaders call these "goals"). We recommend three to six months because this group has a tendency to set long periods for expectations, which, in turn, may create further distance between leaders and stars. Because high performers may need more attention than they typically receive, this shorter period serves as an objective cue for leaders.

Following this, jointly assess any partnerships that may be needed to spur your stars on to further successes. These associations are particularly relevant because organizational stars really need, and excel at tapping into, the talents of others. During this partnership formation stage, specific learning goals may come to the forefront. Discuss these goals with the high performers and identify how to address these needs.

At this point, give your word that you will run interference for them, should they need it. We suggest that you give them carte blanche to offer suggestions on how you might do this for them.

And finally, evaluate and reinforce. Leaders often forget this step because these stars are such independent, successful performers. Let them know how they're doing and invite them to give you periodic updates. During this final phase, remember not to take on the perspective that "no news is good news." If you're not getting periodic updates, check in with the high performers. Be assertive and ask what you could do to help them with their special projects. Doing so will demonstrate that you are an available leader who provides the support and structure needed to truly assist this highly motivated and successful group.

One situation that sometimes arises with organizational stars requires subtlety, and that is when stellar performance falters. It is certainly difficult to maintain such a high level of performance, and some fallout may be inevitable. Here's where you as a leader need to step in and manage the process. Use positive political skills to pave the way for high performers who confront organizational resistance. For example, you may need to smooth some ruffled feathers among the top brass or coach the star on softening his or her curt approach to key individuals within the organization. Whatever it is, you should see this as a stopgap measure that will help these individuals continue their star performance.

Finally, don't underestimate the power of financial rewards. Many leaders are reluctant to consider this because coming up with the money often requires such an organizational juggling act. However, it may be in your best interests—and those of your organization—to act. Consider the heavy costs of recruiting others of this caliber and then getting them up to speed should your high performers leave the organization. We have seen far too many scenarios in which organizational stars who are beginning to feel unappreciated financially end up looking elsewhere. The typical end result: they find other positions, and *then* their current organization, in a last-ditch attempt to keep them, makes a terrific offer that provides the rewards these stars should have been enjoying all along. Sometimes this works, but sometimes it doesn't, so we suggest you show appreciation while you have the chance. Of course, appreciation is more than money, and good relationship building is key, as we note in other sections of this book. But when pay is the issue, the leader needs to act swiftly. Work with your human resources professional to deliver a solution that is equitable for the individual and the organization.

SCENARIO

Managing the Performance of an Organizational Star

Bill, manager of the sales force in an automobile manufacturing company, has a tricky situation on his hands. One of his staff members, Janet, has been a star performer on the top sales team for many years. She has con-

sistently exceeded her sales goals and has coached less experienced team-mates, sharing her strategies for success. Janet has been highly creative in her approach to sales, breaking ground in territories the company never thought could be markets. Others admire and look up to her, and she is proud of her role as a leader among her peers. Janet has a high need for recognition and pins her self-esteem on making her sales goals time and time again.

Last week, however, Janet got word that, for the first time in twenty years, she had not reached her sales target. She responded by lashing out at the sales analyst, accusing him of running the data incorrectly. She created quite a scene and angered the analyst, who defended the numbers and felt his competence was being questioned. The analyst's manager just called Bill to report the incident and ask him to deal with the situation.

Louellen Advises...

Bill, you are encountering an often overlooked aspect of performance management: dealing with a star who has an atypical incident of less-than-desirable performance. Handling this type of situation requires kid gloves since the top performer's ego is often a bit fragile and stars have not had a lot of experience with performance difficulties.

Assume that Janet is well aware that expectations for her have not been met. You do not need to give her extensive negative performance feedback, which may come off as insulting. Rather, help her put the missed sales target in perspective, coaching her on how to recover. Focus on the fact that she has not missed a target in twenty years and that no one can maintain perfect performance forever. Tell Janet you are confident that she will quickly get back on track and help her strategize how she might do so. It may appear condescending if you tell her what to do, so instead ask her what kind of help she would like, allowing her to take the lead. Let her know that you have in no way lost confidence in her abilities and that you are behind her 100 percent.

Mitch Advises...

Bill, the key fact is that Janet has not missed her sales target for twenty years, until now. To me, this signals that this is not necessarily a performance management problem—at least, not the same kind you would confront with a poor performer. There is no pattern of poor performance. Therefore, I would treat Janet as the star she is and use the BRIDGE model we detail in Figure 9.

Focusing on star potential increases the probability that the more recent performance issues will be controlled. I suggest that you brainstorm with Janet regarding her recent accomplishments. Be cautious here. If Janet has achieved star performance, she may ask something like, "OK, Bill, what are you setting me up for?!" If this occurs, respond by explaining that her recent outburst is an issue, but you're actually more concerned with getting her back to her previous star level, and then focus on that. As you review the discoveries Janet has made in the past year, integrate these into expectations for the next three to six months. This could be an excellent time to suggest as one expectation that she maintain her even manner and not lash out at anyone for whatever reason. But don't focus on it. Ask Janet if she needs any partnerships to get her back on track. For example, she may find a partnership through coaching a new salesperson. Remember, to be a leader is to teach. As an added benefit, she may do related tasks better. So ask Janet to select someone with whom she would like to partner and begin sharing her talent with others. Or there may be a particular manager in the area from whom she can learn through an informal partnership, or, as some call it, a mentoring relationship.

You may also wish to have Janet brainstorm with another individual in the organization who is figuring out new ways of bringing in business. Perhaps Janet has been doing this in a face-to-face mode and the other person is having particular success with virtual methods. What a great way for Janet to learn about new methods for improved sales development! You should also determine whether or not you will need to run interference for her. If there's a chance her problem will escalate in the future, you might be able to prevent this from occurring. Finally, let Janet know that you are not going to settle for just being a manager on the sidelines. You want to know how she's doing and would like to get periodic progress reports. Both you and Janet can decide on how frequently these will occur and what the focus should be.

CHAPTER 4

Managing
Conflict

W E OFTEN WONDER WHY managers have such difficulty dealing with conflict. Certainly it represents a threat. Relationships might be damaged, anger could become explosive, and retaliation might result—all outcomes no one wants. Yet, the management of conflict comes with risks, all of which you can mitigate by honing the skills we discuss in this chapter. Both of us live in Minnesota, a state touted for its "Minnesota Nice" phenomenon. This implies that many Minnesotans use a style of conflict management wherein they do not address conflict directly but instead act out their disagreements indirectly by gossiping, avoiding contact, reducing communication, or resorting to innuendo. Even if this is only partially true, we coach our local clients to develop a more forthright style.

PREDICTING ORGANIZATIONAL CONFLICT

Good conflict management begins with prevention. Take a minute to complete Exercise 2, Organizational Conflict Predictor. Your score will tell you how well you have prepared your work environment for effectively addressing the conflicts that are sure to occur. Note that the questions address the need for clear role descriptions, problem-solving processes, and staff members with the skills to communicate in conflict situations. We so often find as we work with our clients that the foundation for conflict resolution has not been laid. Remember the adage "An ounce of prevention is worth a pound of cure."

EXERCISE 2. Organizational Conflict Predictor

Directions: Many organizational conditions can promote or inhibit effective conflict management. Answer the following questions with "Yes," "Somewhat," or "No" in order to determine your organization's chances of managing conflict successfully.

	Yes	Somewhat	No
1. In your organization, is conflict treated as a permissible, resolvable difference of opinion?	☐	☐	☐
2. Do specific channels, informal and formal, exist for managing conflict in a structured manner?	☐	☐	☐
3. Is participative decision making encouraged when important organizational issues are addressed?	☐	☐	☐
4. Do staff members at all levels have effective conflict management skills?	☐	☐	☐
5. Does each employee have an updated job description outlining his or her major responsibilities?	☐	☐	☐
6. Does each department have a clear understanding of its major responsibilities and how they relate to other departments?	☐	☐	☐
7. Are policies written specifically and clearly enough to provide a guide for making decisions that are uniform and fair to all employees and departments?	☐	☐	☐
8. Are staff members willing to collaborate with one another rather than protect their own domains?	☐	☐	☐

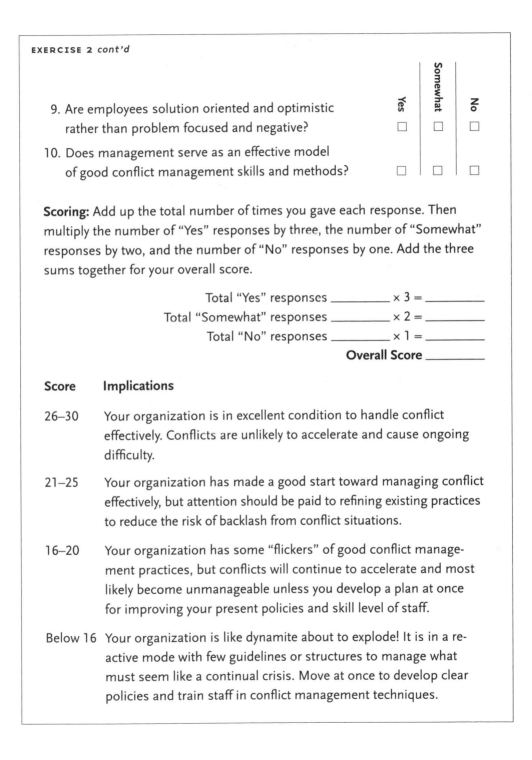

EXERCISE 2 *cont'd*

	Yes	Somewhat	No
9. Are employees solution oriented and optimistic rather than problem focused and negative?	☐	☐	☐
10. Does management serve as an effective model of good conflict management skills and methods?	☐	☐	☐

Scoring: Add up the total number of times you gave each response. Then multiply the number of "Yes" responses by three, the number of "Somewhat" responses by two, and the number of "No" responses by one. Add the three sums together for your overall score.

Total "Yes" responses _____ × 3 = _____

Total "Somewhat" responses _____ × 2 = _____

Total "No" responses _____ × 1 = _____

Overall Score _____

Score	Implications
26–30	Your organization is in excellent condition to handle conflict effectively. Conflicts are unlikely to accelerate and cause ongoing difficulty.
21–25	Your organization has made a good start toward managing conflict effectively, but attention should be paid to refining existing practices to reduce the risk of backlash from conflict situations.
16–20	Your organization has some "flickers" of good conflict management practices, but conflicts will continue to accelerate and most likely become unmanageable unless you develop a plan at once for improving your present policies and skill level of staff.
Below 16	Your organization is like dynamite about to explode! It is in a reactive mode with few guidelines or structures to manage what must seem like a continual crisis. Move at once to develop clear policies and train staff in conflict management techniques.

CHOOSING A CONFLICT MANAGEMENT APPROACH

Begin with determining the best approach for a given situation. Exercise 3, Conflict Management Style Profile, helps you assess your preferred mode of conflict resolution.

EXERCISE 3. Conflict Management Style Profile

Conflict is a pervasive dynamic in most organizations. The manner in which an individual responds to conflict varies in given situations, but one style usually emerges as a preference, particularly under stress.

Directions: The Conflict Management Style Profile presents six situations. Following a description of each situation, five alternative courses of action are listed. Read each situation description and then rank in order (from 5 to 1) on the line provided all five responses that follow.

5 = Most characteristic of your behavior   **1** = Least characteristic of your behavior

When you have completed all six of the situations, record your answers on the scoring grid.

Situation 1
Imagine your current work situation. In most instances, how would you characterize your general orientation to conflicts?

a. _____   Even though I feel strongly about an issue, I'd rather accommodate others than risk damaging relationships.

b. _____   I prefer to avoid taking a position that might perpetuate the conflict.

c. _____   When I feel strongly about something, I want to actively state my position and rarely back off from the opportunity for a good argument.

d. _____   I feel best when I clearly understand all sides of the issue and work cooperatively to meet everyone's needs.

e. _____   I'm willing to give in somewhat, but I expect the other side to do the same.

Situation 2

You are sometimes in a position of authority that gives you more power and influence than others (e.g., a manager or a team leader). When you are the person with *greater* authority, how do you handle a conflict-ridden situation?

a. _____ I do not like to get involved, although I may serve as a facilitator in problem solving to help others maintain amiable relationships.

b. _____ I view myself as responsible if something goes wrong, so I am generally unwilling to forfeit my right to make and implement decisions about what to do.

c. _____ I'm responsible for listening to others and explaining what they may not be aware of. I'm satisfied if everyone gives a little so we can find a middle ground.

d. _____ I take responsibility for getting those involved in the conflict to work together with me and find a way to address everyone's needs.

e. _____ I'm responsible for pointing out the policies and procedures, and if others violate them, then they pay the price.

Situation 3

Professionals are often expected to make decisions by working in teams. When you are working with a team and find yourself disagreeing with other members on important issues, how do you usually respond?

a. _____ I'm sensitive to the feelings of others and try to tone down my remarks so I won't upset anyone.

b. _____ I listen carefully, looking for a compromise solution rather than pushing my own viewpoint too strongly.

c. _____ I try to convince others of the merits of my position.

d. _____ Differences are usually not worth wasting time over, so I don't express myself.

e. _____ I express my viewpoint and actively seek others' opinions as well.

Situation 4

When a peer is angry with you for an action you have taken or a decision you have made and seeks a one-on-one confrontation, what are you most likely to do?

a. _____   I'd avoid having the confrontation for as long as possible.

b. _____   If it would make the colleague happy, I'd probably give in, just to keep the peace.

c. _____   I'd attempt to get all the issues and concerns immediately out in the open.

d. _____   I'd be willing to alter my position somewhat as long as my colleague were willing to do the same.

e. _____   I'd usually be firm in maintaining my position but might agree to meet with my colleague.

Situation 5

When you see a conflict arising between staff members, what do you typically do?

a. _____   I try to soothe their feelings, pointing out the areas of potential agreement between them.

b. _____   I tend to try to avoid direct confrontation and instead steer them toward a middle ground, referring to policies and procedures to break stalemates.

c. _____   I try to forestall the conflict by being humorous or even suggesting the group take a break.

d. _____   I probably take a side on the issue and push to get support from other group members.

e. _____   I attempt to facilitate the communication between them, surfacing feelings and issues in hopes of promoting mutual problem solving.

Situation 6

Decisions of one group in an organization often need to be reconciled with decisions of another group. In selecting a member of your group to negotiate with others, what kind of person would you most likely choose?

a. _____ Someone who will defend our group's positions accurately and will not be intimidated into altering our stance.

b. _____ Someone who could develop a friendly relationship with members of the other group and would not offend them.

c. _____ Someone who could present our group's position skillfully and have equal concern for the other position.

d. _____ A good bargainer who could get some of our group's position incorporated into the final solution.

e. _____ Someone who would avoid participating in conflict and would keep things running smoothly.

Scoring: Transfer to the grid below the number representing your ranking for each alternative in each situation description. *Note:* The letters corresponding to the alternatives do not appear in consecutive order on the grid. After completing the number transfer, add up your rankings for each *horizontal* row.

\	Situation						Total	Conflict Style
1	2	3	4	5	6			
b___	e___	d___	a___	c___	e___		___	Retreat
a___	a___	a___	b___	a___	b___		___	Harmonize
c___	b___	c___	e___	d___	a___		___	Battle
e___	c___	b___	d___	b___	d___		___	Bargain
d___	d___	e___	c___	e___	c___		___	Problem-Solve

Source: Louellen Essex & Associates, 2006

Before reading on, complete the assessment and calculate your score in each of the five categories. The category in which you have the highest score indicates your style preference, and the one with your second-highest number is your backup approach. Table 3 summarizes each conflict management style—retreat, harmonize, battle, bargain, and problem-solve—and outlines the disadvantages and best uses of each.

TABLE 3. Conflict Management Styles and Best Uses

Style	Description/Disadvantage/Best Use
RETREAT	Conflict is not addressed, and withdrawal is the dominant behavior. Conflict is viewed as useless and punishing. The retreater does not pursue his or her concerns or those of anyone else.
Disadvantage:	The conflict can grow to the point that it is not manageable.
Best use:	When issue and timing are not critical.
HARMONIZE	Conflict situations are handled by accommodating the other party. Pursuing an issue is seen as selfish behavior. Maintaining friendly relationships with other people is the prime goal.
Disadvantage:	The source of the conflict rarely goes away.
Best use:	When it is more important to preserve the relationship than to deal with the issue.
BATTLE	Conflict is viewed as a challenging and exciting experience. The individual believes in the correctness of his or her position and actively pursues those beliefs in a competitive fashion.
Disadvantage:	Creates a negative, competitive aftermath.
Best use:	In crisis and when under extreme time pressure.
BARGAIN	Conflict is seen as an opportunity to negotiate, utilizing the idea that "half a loaf is better than none." Bargaining involves willingness to give up something if the other side does, too.
Disadvantage:	Sides often assume inflated positions; solutions may be watered down, resulting in little commitment.
Best use:	When conflict is of moderate importance or when collaboration fails.
PROBLEM-SOLVE	Conflict is perceived as mutual problem solving through which the needs and interests of all parties are equally considered. The goal is to achieve a solution upon which all can agree.
Disadvantage:	If it fails, morale of the group suffers; it's time consuming.
Best use:	To gain support, build trust, and integrate viewpoints.

In determining the most appropriate style for a given situation, consider the time you have available to solve the problem as well as the priority of the issue.

RETREAT

One option you have is to retreat from the situation, doing nothing to address the conflict. This approach makes sense when the issue is of low priority or you determine there is little chance of getting your needs met and your time is best spent on problems on which you can make progress. One of the strategies we have used to help our clients discern the importance of an issue involves a prioritization matrix like the ones we used in Chapters 1 and 2. We hope you appreciate this matrix's flexibility and understand how it can be adapted to a variety of organizational needs. For the purpose of determining whether retreating is the best action, we suggest reconfiguring this matrix, as shown in Figure 10, to evaluate the strength of the need and the probability that the need can be met.

Based on this matrix, leaders would suggest retreating if there were low probability of their needs being met—whether it be a high, medium, or low level of need. We also suggest retreating when there is

FIGURE 10. Prioritization Process Matrix—
Probability of Meeting Needs × Needs Level

	High Probability of Meeting Needs	Medium Probability of Meeting Needs	Low Probability of Meeting Needs
High Needs Level			Retreat
Medium Needs Level			Retreat
Low Needs Level		Retreat	Retreat

a medium probability of needs being met and the need is low, because time invested here is not going to yield a significant return. Interesting to us, leaders sometimes spend an inordinate amount of time determining whether they should or should not retreat. For high needs, this may be time well spent. For anything less, you should consider the benefits and costs of this action and then move on, if warranted.

HARMONIZE

Harmonize when the issue is of greater importance to the other party than it is to you. Why not at times meet other people's needs, focusing on building relationships rather than on getting what you want? When you harmonize, you demonstrate your ability to be flexible and open to others' points of view. Good leaders can be influenced to change their views. Harmonizing is at the center of truly empowering your staff to be part of a decision-making process and lets them know they truly have a voice.

BATTLE

Do battle when you are sure your position is correct. Some types of issues, such as safety, law, and ethics, are simply not negotiable. The leader has to force a solution. Maintaining boundaries of appropriate behavior calls for a strong stance. If you have substantially more knowledge and experience, you can use well-developed persuasion—another form of battling—to win others over to your point of view.

BARGAIN

When a problem is of moderate importance to both parties, bargaining may be the best approach to take. Two modes of bargaining are possible. The first, "split the difference," involves finding a middle ground between two positions. When timelines, finances, and other types of resources are in question, this may be an effective approach. Another type of bargaining, "let's work a deal," involves a trade-off, that is, "I'll do x for you, if you do y for me."

However, we recommend that leaders remain cautious about one consequence of bargaining—what negotiation experts call the "irrational escalation of commitment." When both sides believe their position is correct, they will often fight to the bitter end. The danger here is that by committing too early to the view that your position is correct, you become overly attached to it. This excessive attachment becomes an Achilles' heel when you ignore information that would be in your best interest to accept. In this circumstance, the individual devalues new perspectives brought to the table and becomes more and more irrational in clinging to his or her first and favored position. Leaders can avoid this by staying open to accepting beneficial new information. Likewise, when working with others, leaders should make sure that their staff members follow suit as much as possible.

PROBLEM-SOLVE

Finally, problem solving should be the choice when both parties believe the conflict is important and commitment from both sides is crucial to implementing a solution. Win-win problem solving requires discussing issues from an interest-based rather than a position-based stance. For example, two managers could argue about a conference room they both need, or they could discuss their space requirements and brainstorm options for meeting both sets of needs.

In our experience, and as validated by many large-scale research studies, there are typically multiple interests in any conflict management situation. Therefore, asking both parties to brainstorm their many interests is a key and very successful strategy. At times, people may say that they have only one interest. Don't fall for this! Propel people to go beyond their gut responses and ask them to take time brainstorming all the interests they have. Why? The problem with a position-based stance is that it limits the generation of alternative courses of action. Multiple interests not only serve as a catalyst for the development of multiple action possibilities but also show where trade-offs can occur. For example, a lower-priority interest for one individual may be a higher-priority one for another—the perfect opportunity for a trade-off! We created the decision-making flowchart in Figure 11 to assist our clients in choosing an approach.

FIGURE 11. Flowchart for Choosing One of Five Conflict
Management Approaches

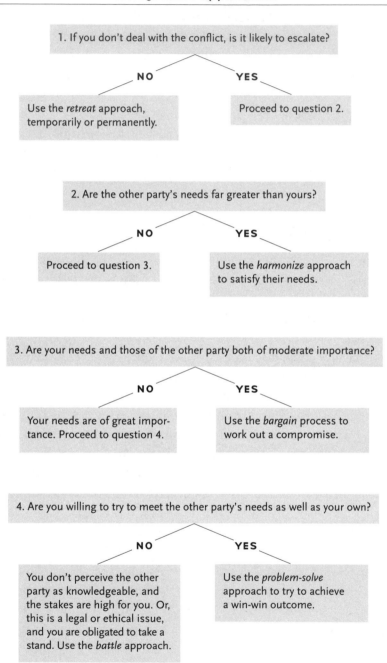

1. If you don't deal with the conflict, is it likely to escalate?

NO

Use the *retreat* approach, temporarily or permanently.

YES

Proceed to question 2.

2. Are the other party's needs far greater than yours?

NO

Proceed to question 3.

YES

Use the *harmonize* approach to satisfy their needs.

3. Are your needs and those of the other party both of moderate importance?

NO

Your needs are of great importance. Proceed to question 4.

YES

Use the *bargain* process to work out a compromise.

4. Are you willing to try to meet the other party's needs as well as your own?

NO

You don't perceive the other party as knowledgeable, and the stakes are high for you. Or, this is a legal or ethical issue, and you are obligated to take a stand. Use the *battle* approach.

YES

Use the *problem-solve* approach to try to achieve a win-win outcome.

COMMUNICATING TO
REDUCE DEFENSIVENESS

The manager's approach to communication throughout a conflict-ridden situation is another important dimension of achieving resolution. As the manager, your goal should be to get the other person to hear your viewpoint and want to cooperate in finding a solution. To achieve this, you must avoid triggering defensiveness, which will shut down the interaction. As we coach clients on how to frame their messages, we often share the following guidelines:

- Describe the problem but don't judge.

- Explain the impact of the problem.

- Request a behavioral or performance change.

- If you can't get agreement, indicate the outcome you desire.

DESCRIBE THE PROBLEM

Describing the problem is your first step. Here, we strongly recommend that you use what we call "behaviorally specific" terms. This reduces the tendency to judge. For example, rather than saying that an individual is not committed to the team because he comes to meetings late, it's far more productive to state that coming late to meetings means that others must take time to bring the person up to speed, which reduces efficiency in the office. See the difference? The former description of the problem is likely to produce a response similar to this one: "Of course I'm committed to the team. Remember how I worked late three times last month?!" The real issue, tardiness, gets lost in the defensiveness about commitment.

EXPLAIN THE IMPACT

Second, you'll need to explain the impact of the problem. Talk about how it's affected you and others. And when you address these issues, be mindful that the other person may have an alternative point of view and be prepared to listen to what he has to say. Don't act based on fixed assumptions. Be sure to check out your assumptions with the person. You may indeed be wrong!

Try not to dig in your heels too deeply. When you explain the issues, avoid using absolute language. For example, rather than saying that the team *always* has to cover for this person or that you can *never* trust him with a new and challenging project, use more behaviorally specific language that truly describes the situation. When we state our views in absolute language, the real issue may get lost in this all-or-nothing language.

REQUEST A CHANGE

Third, request a change in the individual's behavior or performance. Ask the other person to take some actions to resolve the situation. You may want to specify something or leave it in the other person's hands. Whenever feasible, frame it positively. This procedure is based on hundreds of research studies that found more successful results when new behaviors are framed as enhancements instead of as fixes for deficits.

Consider the following scenario. Imagine that you have asked someone to address her organizational skills as related to project management. One way of requesting a change in performance is to ask that person to stop revisiting work that has already been done by other competent staff members. Or you could request that she provide others with the criteria for project success and then ask how she is doing with meeting these criteria. See the difference? Of course, eventually this staff member may have to revisit her poor work on organizing the project but, and here's the key, only after identifying the positive criteria first. In addition, don't assume that you, as the leader, are necessarily responsible for solving the problem. As appropriate, involve staff members in figuring out what changes in their performance are reasonable.

INDICATE YOUR DESIRED OUTCOME

Finally, if you can't get agreement, indicate the outcome you are hoping for. Be the first to say that you were hoping to reach an agreement and that you envision the other party will reconsider. Many clients ask us about issuing an ultimatum. A fair amount of research evidence supports the conclusion that an ultimatum should be the absolute last resort. Instead, build on previous actions that have been successful. Or explain the multitude of benefits that would result from reaching an agreement. Use the ultimatum approach only if you truly intend to follow through on what you say you will do. If not, there is a high probability that you'll be seen as a bluffer and, even worse, a liar. The key message here is that you want to be genuine and trusted in your negotiations because so much is at stake if you become known as a leader who doesn't walk the talk.

DEALING WITH PEERS WHO AREN'T TEAM PLAYERS

This situation comes up often in our consulting practices. It is tricky, because you need to get your peers on your side but don't have the positional power necessary to actively engage them. We looked to some of the most cutting-edge research and practices on negotiation strategies for cues on how to address this dilemma.

The first strategy we suggest is to avoid becoming overly anchored in your preset views before you have had an opportunity to explore them with your peer. All too often, people who are truly committed to a cause are so focused on their own position that they may lose sight of what the other side has to say, views that would be in their best interest to consider. Positional stances force managers into premature judgments and foolhardy errors because their decisions are based on closed-minded perspectives. This leads to the irrational escalation of commitment. By committing to what you want to do without adequately considering what your peer might want or need, you put a stake in the ground and may have difficulty stepping back from it, even when it's irrational. The irrationality becomes even more intense as you defend your view. It causes you to dig in your heels even further, which ultimately affects your judgment. In this situation, you'll likely find extraneous evidence that supports your decision or viewpoint, and this will lead to a poorer decision than the one you might make if you were to keep an open mind. While this can happen in all kinds of negotiation contexts, it's of particular relevance when working with a peer because both of you are at the same level—you have less incentive to listen when negotiating with a peer than when negotiating with someone at a higher level in the organization.

SCENARIO

Dealing with a Peer Who Is Not a Team Player

Bess is a vice president for strategy and research in a midsize New England software development company. New to the organization, she has attempted to keep her colleagues informed on the acquisitions she is charged with making and, in turn, often solicits their input so that she has support for her decisions. What she has experienced is alarming. She has been working diligently on a new acquisition and has asked for counsel from her peers along the way. They said little, so she continued to move forward. Now, at the end of the negotiations to take over the new firm, she has met with resistance from one of her peers, Alex, who is objecting not only to the terms of the contract but to the acquisition itself. Bess is way too far down the track to be able to cancel the deal easily and, more important, she believes the acquisition is crucial to meeting the goals of the company's strategic plan. She is not sure how to proceed.

Louellen Advises...

When a colleague appears to be more focused on a personal agenda than on a team goal, tension soars. Often the person's behavior may shift from a competitive to a collaborative stance. See Table 4 for some descriptors of competitive and collaborative behaviors.

Given that there are other peers involved, your conflict resolution approach should begin with an assessment of whether or not other vice presidents have experienced lack of collaboration with Alex. If so, it makes sense to conduct a group discussion while he is present. If the lack of collaboration is only with you, Bess, the problem is best tackled through one-to-one discussion.

Let Alex know of your concern, using the four communication guidelines given on page 99. Be specific about what you would like him to do differently. Think about the incentives you could emphasize as motivation for working more cooperatively with the group. Attempt to

TABLE 4. Competition vs. Collaboration

Competitive Behaviors	Collaborative Behaviors
Pursuit of own goals	Pursuit of common goals
Secrecy	Openness
Misrepresentation of need	Accurate representation of need
Unpredictable actions	Predictable actions
Threats and bluffs	Negotiation
Irrational perspectives	Logical and innovative perspectives
Focus on stereotypes	Focus on positive feelings

determine what Alex is trying to gain through his behavior. Perhaps he has some real concerns that you should take into account. Or maybe he was more engaged in acquisitions in the past and feels that you are intruding on his territory or haven't sought his expertise enough.

Sometimes lack of cooperation is a form of passive-aggressive behavior. By staying distant and not communicating, Alex may be acting out of frustration and even anger toward you. Left unresolved, these emotions could even lead to active sabotage of your efforts, particularly if he has status in the company. Aim to reduce the appearance of threat you may present. It's critical to move quickly toward having a conversation with him about what you are experiencing and then extending an invitation to work together to improve your relationship.

Mitch Advises...

Something is obviously going on with your peer, Bess. It's not your role to be a diagnostician, but you do need to address the behavior. I suggest you find a course of action that will be a win-win for all, if that's at all feasible. So instead of asking why Alex is doing this, it's probably most effective to deal with his behavior and ask how you can best engage him in moving forward.

I recommend you do this by viewing the situation as a mutual problem-solving paradigm. As such, there is value in assessing the multiple interests you both have. Engage Alex in brainstorming all his interests related to the acquisition. For example, he may be concerned that it will suck the organizational resources dry. Or perhaps that there hasn't been enough due diligence on the acquisition. The one thing to remember is to avoid getting defensive. Force yourself to listen to his concerns. Empathize when you can. And don't interrupt. You can even agree with some of his interests. Agreement can mean that you see the interest as a key concern. And once he's finished talking, make sure he's really raised every interest. Ask him once more if there is anything else he'd like to bring up. Then share your list of interests with Alex. If he starts to interrupt, ask him to extend the same courtesy to you that you extended to him.

You are each brainstorming your own list because extensive research shows that realistic problem solving occurs when multiple interests are addressed. With these interests on the table, you will have your best opportunity to devise a solution upon which all parties can agree. If for some reason you cannot agree, I suggest you take the situation to the entire team.

If you involve the rest of the team, be prepared for some previously unstated trepidations to emerge loud and clear. This is good, though, because you would not want to proceed on something this important without adequately engaging your stakeholders. Use the same process with the group that you used with Alex. Each person should have an opportunity to identify his or her major interests. A little tip in this regard: Be sure to visually summarize everyone's interests by listing these interests on a dry-erase board or flipchart. This tends to speed up the process and helps avoid misinterpretation. If the problem-solving strategy does not work, you may have to bargain—with each side giving up something.

All of this has been a reactive strategy, which is warranted in this situation. In future work with this team, Bess, remember that involvement brings greater commitment, ownership, and results. So think about whether or not you engaged the group adequately before this crisis hit. Perhaps you provided verbal updates and should do it via e-mail. Or maybe you approached the group with the merger idea like a bull in a china shop, and people didn't feel comfortable opposing you at the outset. They might have figured they would speak up at the right time, but the "right time" never came—until now. Whatever the reason, take every opportunity in the future to involve your peers from the start.

ESTABLISHING AN EFFECTIVE WORKING RELATIONSHIP WITH A DIFFICULT BOSS

We remind our clients that there are multiple interests involved in this dilemma—both you and your boss may have valid perspectives. Given this, we ask managers to look at not only their interests but their boss's as well. Create a well-thought-out list of these interests and then prioritize them. When we have done this with our clients, some have discovered that they have a better understanding of their boss's views. This is a benefit of the process, in that it provides a context in which one is more open to considering the many options for achieving a successful working relationship.

Another strategy in working with a difficult boss is to look at your assumptions about the relationship or the work environment. Assumptions sometimes cause us to believe that the other individual (in this case, the boss) will do whatever it is that we fear. Making assumptions based on fears is stress inducing and, sometimes, downright unproductive. So think over the many assumptions you might be making about a difficult boss. Some may be realistic, but others may not be. Weed out those that are likely to be erroneous or, at least, based on false beliefs.

Anger is a normal emotion in conflict situations. But how we deal with it affects the success or failure of the final outcome. Across the board, people tend to respond to anger in a largely ineffective fashion. As consultants, we have seen this as individuals engage in one premature response to anger—dealing with the problem *before* dealing with the person. Essentially, defusing anger successfully is a two-step process:

1. Deal with the person's emotion.

2. Address the problem or issue at hand.

At first, put aside all issues related to addressing the problem. Focus on the person's emotions, acknowledging the anger, with empathy. For example, an effective strategy is to mirror the anger accurately by making statements such as "I understand that you're annoyed" or "You sound really angry." Mirroring is key here because you want to communicate that you perceive the individual's feelings. We have found that, at times, people expend a lot of energy on getting angry and may not want to gloss over it by dealing with the problem prematurely.

We advise our clients to gain a clear understanding of the anger by using language such as "Tell me what it is about the situation that made you so upset." Recognizing the other person's anger also takes some of the wind out of his or her sails so that the focus can shift to the problem. And, by all means, agree whenever you can. You could say, for example, "That must have been a tough way to start your day. Now I understand why you're so upset." And now you're ready to summarize the situation as you understand it, being sure to check your understanding with the other person. Find out what this individual wants you to do. If you're able to do it, super. If not, you may have to negotiate a bit and suggest alternative courses of action.

To effectively defuse anger in others, we recommend avoiding the terms *always* and *never*. Let's say you're about to give someone feedback on her frequent interruptions. You might say something like, "You're always interrupting me." An appropriate response might be, "I'm not always interrupting you. I remember listening to you intently at our last team meeting." Here, the absoluteness of the word *always* has become the issue, and you both become distracted in debating its temporal components instead of the true issue—interrupting.

And what if you are the person who is angry? When your own manager is difficult, the upshot may be that you feel marginalized, insulted, or hurt by behaviors you believe are not respectful of your talent and dedication. Beware, however, of losing control and embarrassing yourself. Instead, take three deep breaths, count to ten, and manage your emotions. And don't send out any e-mails while you're angry. It's fine to write one, but don't type in an address and accidentally hit the send button! If necessary, take a time-out and distance yourself from the situation until you can speak calmly. It may help to reword what your manager said that angered you, using less inflammatory language. Then ask questions to give yourself time to relax a bit before responding. Never mirror the tone and verbiage of the angry person.

We have often given clients who are dealing with conflict situations the Successful Conflict Management Through Negotiation Cue Sheet (see Figure 12), which helps them think through their approach to stressful situations. These guidelines are based on the premise of a win-win nego-

FIGURE 12. Successful Conflict Management Through Negotiation Cue Sheet

In the face of conflict, have you considered:

1. Identifying the other person's interests, not just yours?
2. Using the power of good relationship building before and during the negotiation?
3. Listening first, talking second?
4. Avoiding premature judgments about ideas and people?
5. Framing things as positively as possible? Talking about what can work rather than what won't work?
6. Checking your assumptions about what's being said, or not said, with the other person?
7. Not reacting to emotional outbursts?
8. Not engaging in emotional outbursts yourself?
9. Thinking of solving the problem as a joint effort, focusing on both sets of concerns?
10. Avoiding the irrational escalation of commitment—that is, anchoring yourself in unrealistic options and, as you defend them, becoming more committed to them, as irrational as they may be?
11. Not locking into a position early in the discussion and then finding it hard to back off?
12. Using an ultimatum as a last resort, not as a threat?

---

tiation that stresses trying to satisfy the other person's interests as well as your own. It requires taking a problem-solving approach and not leaping prematurely to solutions before you have a clear understanding of the needs of all parties involved, including your own. For example, saying "I need a 5 percent raise" expresses a position, not an interest. Saying "I don't believe my salary is at market rate" focuses more on your interest and does not lock you into a position too early in the discussion.

SCENARIO

Establishing a Working Relationship with a Difficult Manager

Allen is becoming tired of what he feels is the micromanagement inflicted on him by his manager, Jon. Jon reviews Allen's work in detail, asking countless questions about everything and questioning Allen's decisions. Jon's tone of voice is often stern and a little sarcastic, adding salt to the wound. Allen has come to believe that Jon no longer has confidence in his ability, and he is wondering whether he should take a look at Monster.com. However, he loves his job and the company and would like to find a way to feel successful. Allen has not had performance problems in previous jobs but feels as if he has hit the wall with Jon. The ongoing e-mails Jon sends, which seem intended to document what Allen is supposed to do, or redo, makes Allen feel he has been pegged as a loser. He has been with the company for eleven months and is due for his first performance review next month. Allen wonders how he should approach the issue with Jon and would like to do so before the review.

Mitch Advises...

Well, Allen, you have a touchy situation here, as conflict with the boss is one of the hardest to manage. Looking at the cue sheet in Figure 12, I suggest you'll find the most value in the problem-solving approach of item 9. Think of it as an issue you both need to resolve. As we noted earlier, both parties should be aware there is a problem. Unfortunately, your boss Jon may not yet perceive this issue. Awareness is going to be the first step toward generating a solution.

To begin, then, I suggest you review the communication guidelines on page 99. Jon could become defensive when you bring this up, and you want to reduce the probability that this will occur. For the first step, make sure you are very clear in describing his behavior without expressing judgmental values. For example, if he is redoing your work, tell him that. But don't add that he must be doing so because he doesn't trust you. You don't know this for sure. That's a judgment on your part.

Then let him know what impact this is having on you. It sounds as if you are even thinking of looking for another position. Of course, before you bring this up, you'll have to assess the benefits and risks of such a significant change and of telling him about it. Whatever the impact, be certain that you are honest about it.

Because you are speaking with your boss, you'll also have to step back and listen. Tell him you'd like to hear his views. Take notes. You may actually hear some insights you had not been aware of before. If you are able to act on some of his insights, let him know. This is a great example of what we call "framing." It directs the conflict situation toward the positive by couching your future work in terms of a gain— that you have heard what your boss said and will modify your behavior accordingly. You are framing it positively. However, it's also possible that you may not be able to act on his suggestions.

Next, you need to move on and request a change in his performance. Dangerous? Certainly. But what do you have to lose? You are already thinking of looking for another job. Again, using the framing scenario, offer suggestions for changes he could make in as positive a way as possible. For example, you might request that he provide clearer criteria for you before you start a project. Or that he be open to your sending him sections of a report before the final one is due—just to determine whether you're on the right track. When I worked in industry, I found that being open to receiving projects in installments is a great way to head off potential problems. Perhaps Jon will be amenable to this practice. Give it a try!

And finally, if he won't agree to any of the changes you suggest, at least let him know the outcome you desire. This could include reaching some form of agreement. If you can't get a full agreement, try designing an agreement of different intensities. For example, rather than agreeing that Jon will provide clear criteria all the time, you could both agree that he will provide criteria on those projects you find most challenging. Or ask him if he is willing to sit down with you once a week for an hour and go over all your projects to make certain you understand his expectations. And here's where the different intensities come in: You do this on a trial basis for one month and then both of you reassess the value of this approach.

If you follow these steps, I'm very confident that you will be much closer to having a better working relationship with Jon and will also increase your productivity.

Louellen Advises...

Dealing with situations that involve status and power can be a little trickier. The risk of confrontation may be greater in this situation than in any other, so you must begin with a risk analysis. Ask yourself whether or not your manager has been receptive to open, honest communication in the past and, if so, what the outcome has been. If direct conversation has resulted in a better understanding of each other and a strengthening of your relationship, then go ahead and do what Mitch advises. If you are not sure, ask your colleagues what their experiences have been and seek their counsel on how best to approach Jon. You might also inquire about their experiences with his micromanaging style and what they have done to deal with it.

If you determine that the risk is too great—in other words, that Jon is likely to be punitive if confronted—move to a coping strategy. That means you should abandon the goal of changing Jon's behavior and instead change your approach. Go on the offensive. When discussing an assignment, ask Jon what he needs to see to feel confident that the work was done well. If you've got a long-term project, ask him for a review halfway through to make sure you are on track. When Jon is asking questions and going over what you've done with a fine-tooth comb, manage your emotions by reminding yourself that the behavior is more about Jon than about your performance. Recognize that he is most likely insecure about his own standing in the company and worried that the performance of others will reflect on him if anything goes wrong.

As a last resort, start establishing relationships with other managers in your company and scout out opportunities for a transfer. If another manager becomes impressed with your work, you may be able to get out from under Jon's control. Get involved in company-wide committees and activities, raising your visibility and making contacts. However, don't let others know that you are having difficulty with Jon. Let them discover your talents and whisk you away!

CHAPTER 5

Dealing with Organizational Politics

OR MANY OF OUR MANAGERS, organizational politics is an arena of great mystery. Detecting the complex web of relationships that define the way things really get done presents a daunting challenge, but it is one that any successful manager must meet. It requires uncovering the answers to a set of questions, which will help you determine who holds power and how you can access it. Think of politics not as a negative dynamic, but as a means to gaining power and influence, which will allow you to drive the initiatives that are important to you and your staff. You can mitigate the countless obstacles you will encounter on this quest by applying the investigative techniques we outline in this chapter.

UNDERSTANDING HOW THINGS GET DONE IN YOUR ORGANIZATION

Begin your investigation by answering the questions we present in Figure 13. The flowchart identifies core considerations for dealing with

FIGURE 13. Flowchart for Handling
Organizational Politics

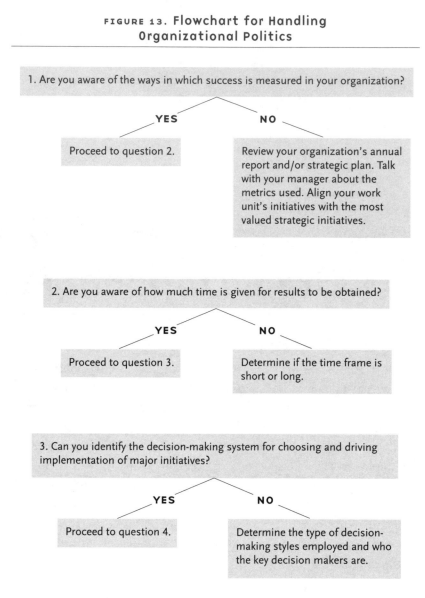

1. Are you aware of the ways in which success is measured in your organization?

YES

Proceed to question 2.

NO

Review your organization's annual report and/or strategic plan. Talk with your manager about the metrics used. Align your work unit's initiatives with the most valued strategic initiatives.

2. Are you aware of how much time is given for results to be obtained?

YES

Proceed to question 3.

NO

Determine if the time frame is short or long.

3. Can you identify the decision-making system for choosing and driving implementation of major initiatives?

YES

Proceed to question 4.

NO

Determine the type of decision-making styles employed and who the key decision makers are.

organizational politics. We have discovered that some leaders refuse to "play politics" and, in so doing, actually limit their base of influence. In this situation, leaders are less apt to comprehend what makes the organization tick.

FIGURE 13 *cont'd*

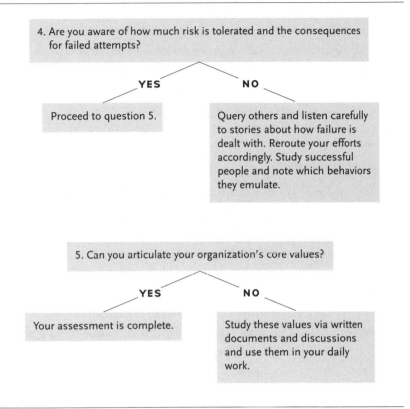

4. Are you aware of how much risk is tolerated and the consequences for failed attempts?

YES — Proceed to question 5.

NO — Query others and listen carefully to stories about how failure is dealt with. Reroute your efforts accordingly. Study successful people and note which behaviors they emulate.

5. Can you articulate your organization's core values?

YES — Your assessment is complete.

NO — Study these values via written documents and discussions and use them in your daily work.

MEASURES OF SUCCESS

Refer to Figure 13 and you'll see that identifying the measures used for gauging success, the focus of question 1, is a key component of understanding organizational politics. What are the most convenient venues in which to locate this information? Try the organization's strategic plan. Its annual report. Performance appraisal forms. Anything that indicates the organization's values and/or its key directions.

As you begin examining these documents, you should be looking for repetition of focus areas—anything that delineates a pattern. These repeated focus areas, which we call data patterns, include such benchmarks as revenue generated, profits acquired, customer retention figures, communities served, and clients helped, just to name a few.

Then, determine how you can align your unit's initiatives with the organization's most valued strategic goals. We have given this assignment to our own clients who need to develop a better understanding of the political contexts that drive organizational momentum. Because politics is linked so critically with people, we recommend that leaders engage others in their units to help identify the alignment between unit initiatives and organizational values. This not only builds political savvy but also cements a foundation for future relationship building.

TIME ALLOTMENT

Next on the flowchart, question 2 asks you to evaluate how much time the organization generally allows for obtaining results. This one often surprises our clients, since leaders typically don't give the issue much consideration. Why? Because they see it as a no-brainer. And no-brainers sometimes get lost in the shuffle, which is why we give it focus here.

If the organization runs on a short-term time frame, your political astuteness will emerge as you tune up the infrastructure in your department so that it moves with lightning speed. For example, you may decide to remove roadblocks that cause sluggish production or processes. Or you could try doing a little less micromanaging. Anything that will put you in sync with the organization's schedule is relevant. If the organization takes more time to obtain results, make sure you provide in-depth information to your team, offer adequate instructions for problem solving, and leave less to chance than would be appropriate for a short-term perspective.

DECISION-MAKING SYSTEM

Question 3 asks about the decision-making methods used for choosing and implementing major initiatives. Table 5 describes some possible methods.

While we understand that no organization typically uses one style, we suggest that you examine your organization's predominant decision-making style or styles. At various meetings in which you are not the leader, assess how decisions are made. Do this as much as you can.

TABLE 5. Methods of Decision Making

Method	Description
Autocratic	Leader decides
Input to leader	Others provide input to the leader, and the leader decides
Consensus	Everyone supports the decision
Input to others	Leader provides input, and others decide
Self-directive	Others decide without leader input

Then start developing a pattern out of what you're observing. You're likely to see one or two basic styles emerge. How does this compare to your way of making decisions? Being politically savvy means patterning your decision-making mode after the organization's style.

Examine, as well, whether individuals or groups review and make key decisions. If there is a highly participative decision-making process, study the behaviors of key members, focusing on how they like to receive information. Know that if a committee structure is involved, decision making is likely to be slower. If driving individuals are at the decision-making hub, the process will be faster. Adapt accordingly. Now you're demonstrating the behavior of a proactive political leader!

RISK TOLERANCE

For question 4 on the flowchart, assess the organization's risk tolerance and the consequences of failure. Organizations that operate at a high risk potential are also going to be more adept at handling failure.

In our national study of leadership failures, which we document in *Breaking the Code of Silence* (Kusy and Essex 2005), we discovered that leaders who are more risk-tolerant allow others to see certain shortcomings—reveal their "human-ness," if you will. In the long run, these leaders are more likely to be successful. This phenomenon has been dubbed the "strategic pratfall effect."

For example, Ann Landers's popularity increased after she announced she was getting a divorce. Communication experts and public relations professionals say she appeared "more human." Psychologists have found that we tend to dislike those who appear perfect because they exhibit the characteristics we most seek in ourselves. More recently, Martha Stewart, who was convicted on charges related to insider trading, used her stay in prison as a stepping-stone to getting her career back on track. Her inmate status softened her intimidating image as a domestic diva. Meanwhile, the value of her company's stock rose substantially following her sentencing in 2004, and up until 2007 she had two shows airing on network television.

As you examine your organization's risk tolerance and failure thresholds, talk to others and listen to stories about how the organization deals with failure. On the one hand, if your organization is risk-averse, establish your own credibility before attempting higher-risk activities. On the other hand, if your organization is more risk-tolerant, you'll discover you'll have more freedom to take measured risks and be rewarded.

CORE VALUES

The final question in the flowchart relates to understanding and modeling the organization's core values. These can include basic tenets such as "patients come first," or "employees are our most important asset," or "quality is our mantra." You'll need to study these carefully to determine if they are simply slogans (in which case you would not give them as much attention) or true values, which need to be modeled. Show your political wherewithal by referring to these values in e-mail messages, in the documents you produce, in the contributions you make at meetings, and in performance management discussions with staff members.

CREATING A BASE OF INFLUENCE AND LEADERSHIP POTENCY

One aspect of your political analysis is to determine which personal bases of influence will allow you to make an impact.

Many behavioral scientists have identified the ways in which individuals gain power in groups. When others view you as someone with valuable knowledge not available elsewhere, you have *expert* power. If you can grant others the things they want (e.g., recognition, promotions, opportunities for involvement), then you have *reward* power. *Coercive* power, when you can take away from others the things they value (e.g., by reprimanding, firing, or withholding assignments and opportunities), is just the opposite. Any individual in a managerial position has both reward and coercive capabilities. You have *connection* power when you have a strong network of relationships that allows you to get things done more readily and, through the informal communication hub in your organization, keeps you well informed by giving you access to information that is not passed through formal channels. *Referent* power comes when you are liked and respected and have a reputation as a good leader with whom people want to work.

Determine which of these power bases you now possess and then work to develop the ones that will strengthen your influence with others. Beware of overusing coercive power, for obvious reasons!

ALLIANCES AND COALITIONS

Yet another complex element of organizational politics concerns alliances and coalitions. Be careful. If you align too strongly with one faction, you will certainly alienate other factions, which could work against you if there's a political upheaval. We advise our clients to develop a broad foundation of relationships that will give them strength throughout the ups and downs of organizational life.

One area of coalition building that often perplexes leaders is handling those who staunchly oppose them. Inappropriate and ineffective actions include engaging in passive-aggressive behavior or ignoring these individuals. In contrast, one action that has tremendous value is working with, not against, the opponent. To do this, you, as the leader, need to spend time with the other person. While some of your effort should be focused on helping the individual understand your view, you should allot an equal amount of time to understanding the other party's view. This approach has three purposes. First, it will increase your knowledge about the issue and provide a context for making better decisions. Second, you may actually change your point of view as a result of this new information. And third, if you can win over an opponent, he or she may become one of your most enthusiastic supporters. By achieving these three goals, you will likely be viewed as a builder rather than a destroyer of supportive relationships. People have a tendency to identify more with builders than with fighters. In this situation, you're operating as a proactive leader who uses positive political networks to achieve your goals.

SCENARIO

Creating a Base of Influence and Leadership Potency

Janice has just accepted a new position, running international operations for a midsize medical device company that specializes in artificial joints used by orthopedic surgeons. She has worked in the industry for many years and within her current company for the past five. Janice is unknown to most of the seventy-five staff members in her work unit, although her reputation is positive throughout the company and within the industry.

She is worried, however, about a potential threat to her effectiveness in her new role. Bob, one of three candidates who applied for her position, will be reporting to her, and he is angry about being passed over. He does not think Janice has the international experience to lead the staff, while he is sitting on fifteen years of successful worldwide sales work, including seven in management. He sees her as a "lightweight" when it comes to what he believes is the rough-and-tough world of the international marketplace. Bob has made it known to the other managers who report to Janice that he does not think she is fit for the job, and he appears to be actively sabotaging her. Janice needs to develop a strategy to deal with her opponent.

Louellen Advises...

In my experience, Janice, almost every leader working his or her way up the corporate ladder encounters a "Bob." I call these characters "organizational bullies" because they have learned to muscle their way into the positions they want. You will have to proceed with drive and confidence in order to counter the effects of Bob's antics. Remind yourself that your track record is just as strong as Bob's and that you were put into your new position for a reason: you are viewed as someone who can do the job. Just because Bob has several years of international experience does not necessarily mean that his experience is relevant to today's situation. You may be seen as more current, with a better leadership style for the staff in the work unit. Start your tenure by interviewing each of your staff members and asking them three questions:

- What is going well in the work unit that you would like to maintain?
- What can be improved in the way the work unit operates?
- What changes would you like to see made?

Additionally, review all documents relevant to the business of international operations and then set up a meeting with the managers. Review your assessment of the work unit and its key initiatives. Talk about your background and approach to leadership. Inspire them to want to move forward on the path you have outlined by promising to engage them in the process. Identify some sure hits—quick results that will help you establish a track record and gain even more credibility.

If Bob continues to actively sabotage you, call him into your office and have a conversation with him. Let him know you are well aware of what he is doing and that you expect him to work with you even though he wanted your job. Assure him that you will use his talents in return for his cooperation. Make it clear, however, that you are in charge!

Mitch Advises...

Janice, I often see this dilemma in organizations where individuals vie for scarce resources—in this case, a key position. I advise that you largely ignore Bob's barrages and attempts to throw you off kilter; you do need to be politically savvy, but not with him. You need to find the right context for this. And the right place to focus your energies is with your team, not Bob.

Review the questions in Figure 13 and you'll discover several areas that may provide you with political mileage. Go on a search mission and ask your staff members some of these questions. Get a feel for how this unit operates. With this approach, you'll accomplish two things. First, you'll obviously uncover the pulse of the unit. Second, you'll likely be perceived as a leader who values the input of others.

If these strategies don't bring Bob's behavior down to at least the level of nonresistance, then you'll need to forget the political arena momentarily and adopt a performance management mode—stating your expectations, monitoring performance, and providing feedback accordingly. At this stage of the game, kick into your directive mode, let Bob know what you will and won't tolerate, and then stick to reinforcing appropriate behaviors and disciplining nonproductive ones.

GAINING CREDIBILITY AND RECOGNITION FOR YOU AND YOUR STAFF

Building your credibility will require developing a track record of success that is known throughout your organization. Some leaders shy away from this kind of fanfare, believing that others may see the behavior as a form of "tooting one's own horn." However, there are many contexts where it is appropriate. Meetings and one-on-one conversations are perfect venues to let your knowledge and competency be known in subtle ways. For example, by offering relevant information, good ideas, and creative solutions to the issues at hand, you will become known as someone with talent. To further your credibility, make sure you and your staff members measure success in attaining the goals you set. Metrics will allow you to provide strong evidence of your value and further establish yourself as a leader worthy of recognition.

Don't stop here. For others to know of your success, it is often necessary to make them understand what you have accomplished. Share the good work of the unit you lead whenever the opportunity arises. Don't assume your successes will be noticed. You might do this in a number of ways, such as offering to report at meetings, submitting stories of your work unit's accomplishments to your organization's publications, and publicly recognizing individuals who report to you for specific achievements. Think of yourself as a public relations agent for you and your work unit.

SCENARIO

Gaining Credibility and Recognition for You and Your Staff

Mark cannot believe what just happened. In an all-staff meeting of the public works department, which he manages for the city, the speaker announced that a major construction project had been successfully completed. Several people were acknowledged as responsible for the outcome, but Mark and his staff were left out. Mark knows that the project would have failed without his team. They troubleshot many major crises so that project timelines could be maintained. Mark is furious, but he knows he must be careful not to let his anger get the best of him. The omission is especially hard to swallow because it has happened before. The division director has a way of taking most of the credit for all of the good things that happen, only occasionally acknowledging those in his inner circle. Mark knows he cannot continue to let this happen without trying to do something about it. His staff's morale is sinking because of the lack of appreciation from upper leadership. What should he do to address the issue?

Mitch Advises...

Mark, you're in a double bind here. The division director is your boss's boss, so you know you must tread lightly. Yet, you and your staff have not received the acknowledgment you deserve. What makes matters worse is that this is not the first time this division director has neglected to mention your and your staff's achievements. You may find it useful to review the section on creating a base of influence earlier in this chapter. It's obvious that the division director is operating from a base of coercive power and you (and your team) are functioning from the perspective of expert power. I don't think you are going to get him to rectify his taking credit for the project.

Instead, I recommend that you focus your energy on connection power. You have strong relationships with many constituencies in the city. Schedule a meeting with one of these individuals who knows of your team's superior work and who has political savvy. Ideally, but not necessarily, this person would be your boss. Help this individual understand the work you have done and seek ideas on how to showcase it. Don't mention the division director's name. Keep this casual and proactive. Then, ask this key connector if he or she would be willing to contact others who could provide a venue for highlighting your group's work.

Now, here's the sensitive part of this endeavor. What should you do if the division director finds out (which he undoubtedly will)? Avoid the reactive mode by considering the proactive. This means that you should invite the division director to this showcase of your staff's results. Give him credit for as much as seems right to you and your team. Make sure that your connector has the political clout to withstand any backlash that may occur and, even more important, is regarded positively throughout the organization and can bear witness to your group's outstanding work. And finally, if this connector is not your boss, find ways to involve your boss in the process. Remember, involvement is critical in that it helps build commitment and better outcomes!

Louellen Advises...

Mark, I suspect you may not be tooting your own horn or that of your staff quite enough. One important political skill is being a good public relations agent for your work unit. Stand back from your frustration about the current situation and ask yourself how often you have made others aware of your staff's important role in projects. You might do this in casual as well as formal one-on-one conversations with key people and in meetings, where you have a more public forum. Congratulate your staff through e-mail and copy your own manager, and maybe even the division director, if your manager approves. Consider writing a brief article for the company's Web site or newsletter, describing your group's accomplishments and giving credit to specific individuals.

What I am saying here, Mark, is that you shouldn't assume the division director is deliberately leaving you out. It is possible he's just unaware or inattentive. In organizational communication, there is a concept called the "mum effect." As leaders move further up the organizational structure, they typically become more removed from what is going on in the organization. They rely on others to give them information, unless they're among the few who make a strong attempt to get it themselves. As you develop your network further and gain more allies, you will most likely discover that others will deliver the message of your staff's accomplishments.

You also have to confront the issue of how to work through your staff's disappointment at not being recognized. I think it is important to meet with staff members, to let them vent and to give you a chance to demonstrate your own disappointment and empathy. Be ready to offer them a plan of action for making their work more visible. Be sure they know that you value all that they do and see them as members of a team of high achievers.

CHAPTER 6

Establishing Yourself as a New Leader

A **NEW MANAGER IS THE FOCUS** of staff members' hopes and fears—hope that the work environment will be improved and problems will be solved, and fear that things might worsen, putting careers at risk. A new leader often upsets the equilibrium of existing procedures, either consciously or unconsciously. Even if things weren't the greatest with a group's previous leader, many team members would opt for maintaining the status quo instead of rocking the boat, because the latter might make things worse, not better. These are some of the rather daunting challenges many new leaders face. At the same time, the new manager harbors a parallel set of hopes and fears—including hope that he or she will be successful and create a high-performing, highly recognized work unit, and fear that insurmountable challenges will emerge.

The transition to a new leadership role must be handled with care. We are often surprised that some organizations within which we consult do so little to assist a new manager. Promotion is based more on technical expertise, without enough emphasis on the human skills needed to motivate staff members to achieve their best work. Organizations rarely develop a structured process that eases the transition, so the new kid on the block is often left to his or her own devices. Think about the last time you were new to a leadership position. Were you more concerned about the "what," the content of the job, or about the "how," the process by which the work gets done? In our experience, we have discovered it's typically the latter. Most new leaders give a lot of thought to such things as fitting into the culture, connecting with the values of the organization, and accomplishing key goals through the team.

This chapter offers advice on two important process elements of establishing yourself as a new leader: developing an approach to entering a group as a new leader, and dealing with peers and others who do not support you.

DEVELOPING AN APPROACH TO ENTERING A GROUP AS A NEW LEADER

Now that you've been given the new job or promotion, where do you begin? Our first piece of advice: Don't move too quickly to critique, make changes, or promise anything.

One of the themes we emphasize here is the importance of putting people first as a contributor to leadership and organizational success. Documented evidence affirms the value of relationship building as a precursor to successful organizational outcomes. This applies to all leaders, especially new ones. For example, one study after another has provided concrete evidence that there is a direct correlation between an organization's success and leadership practices that treat people as assets. After all, it's only common sense. Then why do many new managers disregard this evidence and focus too much on the tasks at hand? We believe this is directly attributable to the fact that tasks are easier for some than "touchy-feely" relationship building. So if you're a new leader who is using your first few weeks to really understand the people you're working with, kudos to you! Don't let up. And if you happen to be a more task-driven leader, just remember that the appropriate time for tasks will come later. Focus first on the real task at hand—understanding your key stakeholders.

For those who basically agree but still might doubt the prominent place these relationship-building perspectives hold, consider another research study that might make a believer out of the most die-hard task-focused leaders. This study of 968 organizations representing all major industries found that high-involvement and high-commitment work practices are associated with a 7.05 percent decrease in turnover and $27,044 in increased sales per employee as well as $18,641 more in market value and $3,814 in profit, both again per employee (Huselid 1995). Stated another way—in an organization of one hundred employees, engaging in this approach will yield increased sales of $1,864,100. Now, we're certainly not suggesting that these are the kinds of results you will always obtain, because there are many intervening variables. But numerous studies indicate that an organization will get further ahead by engaging its workforce. And what better way for a new leader to start than by demonstrating this!

Some new leaders have told us that some of the more autocratic organizations don't support this relationship-building perspective. We adhere to the premise that blaming it on the organization is not an excuse. In small ways, even a new leader can go against the organizational grain to forge an effective leadership path with a new team.

Consider what Harvard researcher Debra Meyerson (2001) discovered about "tempered radicals," who bring about change the quiet way—even when they do not have support from the rest of the organization. For example, one stressed-out manager decided to arrive at work a bit earlier, take lunch breaks (something the organization frowned upon), and refuse most evening business calls. Remarkably, this leader's performance improved, and others then followed suit. Our point here is that just because a particular management practice is not common doesn't mean a new leader has to avoid it. We say this in response to those leaders who believe that their organizations want them to begin the "real work" immediately. Leaders can certainly shorten the process time by abbreviating interviews with key stakeholders, spending less time discussing themes, and providing selected information via e-mail instead of in person. But they absolutely should not just forget the process completely and focus only on the content of the job. All the evidence strongly advises against doing this.

Figure 14 presents a guide to making the transition to your new leadership role.

FIGURE 14. Flowchart for Assuming
Your New Leadership Role

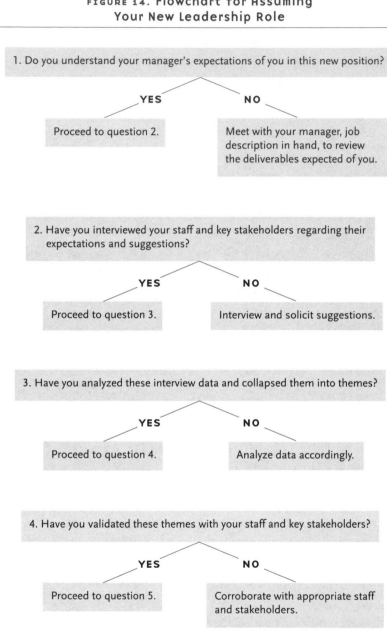

1. Do you understand your manager's expectations of you in this new position?

YES   **NO**

Proceed to question 2.   Meet with your manager, job description in hand, to review the deliverables expected of you.

2. Have you interviewed your staff and key stakeholders regarding their expectations and suggestions?

YES   **NO**

Proceed to question 3.   Interview and solicit suggestions.

3. Have you analyzed these interview data and collapsed them into themes?

YES   **NO**

Proceed to question 4.   Analyze data accordingly.

4. Have you validated these themes with your staff and key stakeholders?

YES   **NO**

Proceed to question 5.   Corroborate with appropriate staff and stakeholders.

FIGURE 14 *cont'd*

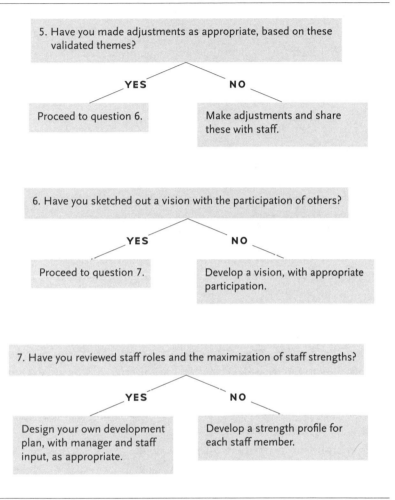

OBSERVE, LISTEN, AND ASSESS

In the first phase of your transition, observe and listen, making a measured assessment of what has just landed in your lap. Begin by meeting with your manager to make sure you understand what is expected of you. Ask what deliverables are expected. We hope your boss will talk with you about his or her expectations of you as a new leader. Make sure these are as concrete as possible so that they can be clearly executed.

Then review all documents relevant to the work of your group, as well as of the organization, if it's new to you, and begin interviewing your staff and those stakeholders with whom you will be interacting frequently. Ask them what is going well that they would like to maintain, what weaknesses they perceive in the way the work unit operates, and what changes they suggest. These interviews don't need to be formal; instead, think of them as opportunities for you to garner the information you need to succeed in the position. Consider not only people's expectations but also their suggestions. Use these as relationship-building venues, providing contexts for future resources.

ESTABLISH YOUR CREDIBILITY

After you have gathered the information, take time to analyze it and develop some themes in preparation for meeting with your new staff and making your official debut. Don't overload them with information—just high-priority themes. It's key here that you not merely present these themes but rather validate them with your staff. See the difference? In the former, you're operating in a "tell" mode, which, as you are new to the organization, may be construed as grandstanding or insensitivity. Remember, this group has been around for some time, and you need to learn from them before they can learn from you! This is your opportunity to validate what you have heard and adjust your interpretations, if warranted. Have a dialogue about what these themes mean. Seek input on how you might deal with some of the more critical issues that emerge. One precaution here: Don't promise anything unless you are sure you can deliver. The only thing worse than a leader in the tell mode at this stage is the inauthentic leader who promises more than is realistic.

Share your observations with your group and outline your vision for a future direction. But make sure it's just an outline. You may recall what we noted in Chapter 1 in the section on strategic planning: the best visions are participative. As you sketch out this vision, see if it resonates with them. What's missing? What particular challenges are associated with it? Be open with group members about what will be involved in any final vision. But don't go too far by discussing the complexity of the process and all the extra work they'll have to do. The bottom-line message you want to impart is that you will engage them as much as possible as you move forward in running the department.

Group members will be very curious to know more about you beyond anything that a résumé or the interviews you have already conducted may have revealed. Tell them more about your background and how you hope to use your talents in your new leadership role. Remember that you are in the process of establishing your credibility. If, in your interviews, you uncovered some major problems with work procedures, beware of stepping on the toes of the senior staff who may be wedded to current operations. Give credit to those who went before you for laying a foundation upon which everyone can build.

ENGAGE TEAM MEMBERS IN RESOLVING AN ISSUE

Search for some quick hits—problems you can readily solve alone or with others. Remember the power of engagement. So although you may find solutions to some problems on your own, be sure to use the talents of your team to address others. For guidance on selecting which issues to confront, we suggest that you review the prioritization process matrix on page 16 and start with the items that have the greatest organizational impact and will require the least amount of resources to correct.

Staff members like to see a leader who can make things happen, and that's exactly what you want to demonstrate. You might, for example, use your expertise to solve a lingering technical problem, acquire a desired and necessary piece of equipment, or fill a vacant position. Be careful not to take on significantly more than you can handle. Some leaders make this mistake. They want to please at this early juncture and take on too many complex tasks that are beyond their expertise. Please note that by *expertise* we mean here not a leader's ability but his or her understanding of process variables such as the group's norms, the organization's culture, and the lingering effects of the previous leader's tenure.

APPRECIATE GENERATIONAL DIFFERENCES

If you are a younger person and your new group includes several older staff members, work hard to draw them into your decision-making process, acknowledging their experience. Put yourself in their shoes, recognizing that it may be difficult to take direction from someone the age of their children. Our experience says to take a collaborative, rather than a directive, stance in your leadership style and remain respectful of the wisdom of individuals of all ages.

We have documented much about the process of working with different generations in *Fast Forward Leadership* (Essex and Kusy 1999). Our research indicates that generational influences abound. For example, documented evidence shows that we have never had so many executives age thirty or younger. This presents special challenges to younger leaders as well as the team members they lead. Likewise, we have never had so many traditionalists (age sixty-five and older) in the workforce. Leaders—both very young and seasoned—face particular challenges because they run smack into the stereotype of the "ideal" age for a new leader. For example, while conducting a research study on the number of traditionalists achieving renowned status, we learned some tradition-zapping facts. In one of the organizations we researched, Texas Refinery Corp., 55 percent of their top sales associates were sixty-one to eighty-one years of age. When we interviewed CEO Jerry Hopkins in 1999, he said, "We're not a company of older salespeople; we simply welcome them." So if you are a leader who doesn't fit the stereotype of a leader, you'll need to take even more time to engage people by seeking their advice, polling their views, and checking your assumptions with them. In particular, if you're a young leader with older staff members or an older leader with many young staff members, you'll need to understand the dynamics inherent in these potentially volatile situations.

ASSESS ABILITIES AND PERSONALITY TRAITS

Once you have a firm sense of the group's norms, start assessing the abilities and personality traits of your staff members and deciding whether or not they are maximizing their talent in their current roles.

The best managers play to the strengths of the individuals they lead, placing them in positions that minimize their weaknesses. You may discover a need to reorganize, but we suggest a bit of caution here. Some new leaders want to reorganize too quickly. We wish we had a dollar for every leader who asked us to help reorganize his or her work area! Resist the temptation to reorganize before you truly understand the unit and the capabilities of staff members.

As you evaluate your staff, think about your own talents. If this is your first management role, you may discover that you are ill-equipped to handle some aspects. Work on your own development plan and search out a mentor who can give you advice and share personal experiences. Attend classes to crank up your skill set. Observe and learn from effective leaders within your organization. This is probably a good time to interview staff members and key leaders again. This time, though, focus on what you have learned and the changes you have made. Listen to what they think about what you have accomplished. Use these reflections for future learning and to guide actions that both you and your team will undertake.

CREATE STAFF DEVELOPMENT PLANS

One way to make sure you are in touch with the needs of your new staff is to create a development plan for each person, or review the plans that are already in place. The following questions will help you in preparing to develop your staff's talent.

- Are you clear about performance expectations for each person you manage?

- Do you have a sense of the development opportunities staff need in order to meet the expectations?

- Do you know what your staff's career aspirations are?

- Can you inspire others to commit to their development by encouraging, supporting, recognizing, and conversing?

- Are you aware of an array of learning/development opportunities available within and outside the organization?

- Do you have a way of assessing the strengths and growth needs for each person you would potentially coach?

- Have you mastered the communication skills of critical feedback, specific praise, and active listening?

- Can you use yourself as a role model?

- Do you know how to teach a specific skill, behavior, or way of thinking?

- Do you know how to create a learning environment?

- Have you thought about the political skills staff may need in order to succeed in your organization? Can you give advice on how to master those skills?

- Do you network staff with individuals, organizations, and resources that may help them build their careers?

- Do you serve as an advocate for your staff in the broader organization?

- Do you see coaching as an important part of what you do? Do you make time for your staff?

We realize you may not have all the answers if you are new to your role; in that case, keep the questions in the back of your mind, as a reminder.

FIND A MENTOR

As you make the transition to your new role, consider seeking guidance from a mentor. Determine beforehand the areas in which you would like the mentor's assistance. Your goals might focus on the following sample areas:

- Understanding how your organization is structured and why

- Acquiring technical expertise in all or part of the area you are managing

- Being more aware of those with whom you must interface in order to get things done

- Identifying learning opportunities within the organization and your profession

- Thinking through approaches to specific issues or problems you have acquired

- Developing a career path

- Assessing and managing your staff talent

Once you have identified what you want to achieve through a mentoring relationship, go in search of a suitable person. Consider proposing that you meet this individual periodically, so you may observe him or her in action. Or, have the person observe you doing something, such as facilitating a team meeting, and then provide feedback. We have found that active observations are even more effective than ongoing conversation in accelerating the learning curve. The great thing is that a mentor is not your manager, which makes it easier to accept feedback without worrying about being judged.

SCENARIO

Making the Transition to a New Leadership Role

Sonja, a new graduate from a prestigious MBA program, has landed her first leadership role in information services at a health care center. Sonja worked in IS for two organizations before going back to graduate school. She led several large projects and gained some practical leadership skills through those experiences. She was a star student and was hired with high expectations that she would quickly grow to be a key leader in the organization. With a twenty-person staff and two supervisors reporting to her, Sonja is both excited and anxious as she faces many challenges: multiple demands from many departments for technological solutions to support patient care coupled with the need for her staff to upgrade outdated software.

Sonja would like some advice to help her develop a strategy for managing her transition. There are several senior staff people in her group, and she is aware that some see her as a young whippersnapper. She knows she will have to move quickly to gain their respect.

Louellen Advises...

First, Sonja, know that you are entering the role with an excellent background in terms of education and experience. Proceed with confidence and focus on how you will go about putting your signature on the department's work by eliminating the problems you have been charged with fixing. Don't worry much about the age difference between you and senior staff. Sometimes experience in the IS area is not entirely useful, given the rapid pace of technological change. You most likely bring fresh, up-to-date skills that can help everyone move IS forward.

Present your staff with the technical challenges you face. Work with them to develop an approach and a work plan. Assess their technical skills and make assignments that are a good match for their abilities and will give them a chance to learn new skills. Show respect for their experience and ask for their advice. Don't be arrogant.

At the same time, you will need to develop relationships with managers in the patient care areas who are your stakeholders. Meet with them, develop a clearer understanding of their needs, and let them know what you plan to do to solve the problems they are facing. In essence, you must build collaboration in two arenas: with your staff and with your new colleagues.

I suspect, too, that you will have to be a quick study on health care if this is a new arena for you. Learn all you can about the industry so that you will be able to participate in discussions and demonstrate the background knowledge that will give you credibility. Read journals, attend conferences, query others in the organization. You must move fast to get the knowledge necessary to be viewed as credible.

Last, I would advise you to find a wise, senior member of the organization who will serve as your mentor. Let this person give you counsel on the politics of the organization and help you work through the day-to-day challenges of being a new leader.

Mitch Advises...

Before you do anything, Sonja, make sure you take time to understand the needs of your work group. Find out about their past successes. Their stumbling blocks. Their views on how to propel the team to future successes. Then take time to discuss some of their insights as well as yours.

Use their reflections as a backdrop for what the department might do in pursuit of even more effective performance. And be sure to recognize the team for its previous good work, which occurred before you arrived on the scene.

Then find ways to slowly integrate some of your approaches. For example, if you're typically a consensus builder, use this strategy and be sure to name what you are doing. Naming your actions as consensus building will help staff members identify your approach, and they may try it themselves! I have also found that when people name something, they become better at doing it. Years ago, when I was head of leadership development at American Express Financial Advisors, we brought in key leaders to cofacilitate training with the leadership development staff, and many leaders discovered that they became better at what they had taught. They understood what they were doing better because they had names for the strategies they were using. Naming what you're doing is one of the ways in which you, as a new leader, can teach. Think of other vehicles for teaching as part of your leadership venue.

Finally, be sure to include your boss in what you're doing. Involve him or her in the challenges you are facing. Sometimes, new leaders are reluctant to talk about the problems they are experiencing or have a tendency to downplay their difficulties with their bosses. Don't succumb to this! The steep learning curve phase of your tenure is the best time for engaging your boss in these kinds of discussions.

Try these approaches, and I'm sure your previous record of success will shine through. Good luck, Sonja!

DEALING WITH PEERS WHEN PROMOTED FROM WITHIN

New managers have often sought our advice upon being promoted to lead their peers in a work group. The move from peer to leader of former peers can be a tough one. Even if the new leader has been the informal leader of the group, the dynamics change when he or she assumes a formal leadership role.

Why does the tension mount? With the formal role comes the ability to use coercive power, something we discussed in Chapter 5. The new leader is now in a position both to take things away, such as salary, desired work assignments, and status, and to dole out rewards. Given that each member of the work group has a history with the newly promoted peer, they all worry that negative events might be used against them. Biases, as well as previous loyalties and constituencies, come into play.

The flowchart in Figure 15 provides some questions to address when promoted from within.

FIGURE 15. Flowchart for Dealing with Peers
When Promoted from Within

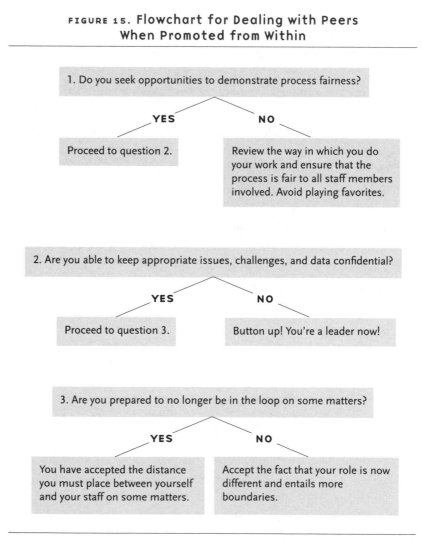

PROCESS FAIRNESS AND OUTCOME FAIRNESS

The issue is one of fairness: Can the new leader look beyond past events and focus only on the performance of individuals? It's incumbent upon the new leader to emerge as one who is fair on all counts. For you to be regarded as such, we suggest you first consider the concept of fairness in a new light. We have consulted with leaders who have been in this relatively common predicament and helped them understand the difference between process fairness and outcome fairness.

Process fairness, according to Columbia University Business School professor Joel Brockner (2006), does not typically involve getting what you want. Rather, it's about providing opportunities for addressing both your views and the views of others. When this occurs, results are more likely to be positive. Outcome fairness, in contrast, relates to employees' judgments about the results of their exchanges with employers.

Process fairness carries the most weight. Consider what Brockner has to say about a study of approximately one thousand individuals conducted by researchers E. Allan Lind and Jerald Greenberg. The primary indicator of whether an employee sues the organization for wrongful termination is his or her view on the fairness of the termination procedure. The following statistics present an expansive view of this process of fairness. Approximately 1 percent of terminated employees who believed they were treated with fairness filed a wrongful termination lawsuit, but 17 percent of those who felt they were not treated with process fairness filed a wrongful termination suit.

So what do these data have to do with the leader who is promoted from within? We think plenty. A newly promoted leader who provides opportunities for process fairness is likely to be more successful than one who provides only outcome fairness. Consider this situation. A newly appointed leader takes time to share his or her concerns about what it's like to be promoted from within, admits the difficulties involved in making decisions that will affect his former peers, and hears the concerns of the others. This leader has a higher probability of being successful than does a leader who sweeps these concerns under the rug. Outcome fairness would focus instead on this leader being fair in such areas as assessing performance, distributing rewards, and providing enhanced benefits. Not that these are insignificant. The point we are making, however, is that leaders who have been promoted from within will be further ahead if they focus on both process fairness and outcome fairness—exponentially so.

CONFIDENTIALITY

Once you have demonstrated process fairness, you're ready to move on to the second aspect of promotion from within—confidentiality. This is a key group dynamic facing a new leader. Before, participation in office gossip was most likely part of everyday work life, but now it must stop. This is the time to realize that you are in a new role among old cronies. Leaders must button up when it comes to bad-mouthing the organization and individuals. The new leader's former peers will be less comfortable talking openly, unsure of how their informal conversations may be judged. So casual communication is often stilted at first, although conversations will likely flow more freely in time. But you must avoid the temptation to give up even a little confidentiality in the hope that you will be seen as more of a team player. Giving away confidential information, no matter how trivial, is likely to set you up for future failure as a leader.

SCENARIO

Dealing with Former Peers
When Promoted from Within

Beth has worked in the customer service area of a direct marketing company for many years. She has a track record of consistently high performance and is known to have a no-nonsense demeanor, focused on getting the job done, sometimes at the expense of her peer relationships. Beth has strong family values and works hard during the day so that she can devote herself to her children and husband during her off-work hours. Consequently, she has not participated in many of the informal social activities along with the rest of her peers. Her dedication to the company and her results orientation have recently been rewarded with a promotion, and she is now the manager of her department.

Her seven former peers, viewing Beth as a goody two-shoes, are acting a little cool toward her. They imagine she will require more of them, raising

standards and tightening up some of the work rules with which they have
been known to take liberties. Beth wonders how she can gain their respect
as she makes the transition to her new leadership role.

Mitch Advises...

Beth, you have so much going for you in terms of your previous record of success. You're now in a leadership position, and you may have to change your stance on how you approach your job. Previously, you were an individual contributor and, as such, could work on your own much more than you probably will be able to do now. It is fascinating to me that your former peers fear that you are going to require more of them. Based on the "old" Beth, this may be true. However, that was the individual contributor Beth. Now we're talking about the leader Beth.

In this new leadership role, you're going to have to consider the value of relationship building more than you ever have before. For example, like it or not, you need to do more socializing. I am certainly not saying you should lessen your standards on work expectations. Rather, you will likely see the value in coaching others, listening to their needs, acknowledging accomplishments, and, yes, attending special events like annual recognition awards ceremonies and perhaps even accepting invitations to personal events. Obviously, you will choose which ones to attend within the framework of your busy professional and personal schedule. Participate in those that are most meaningful to you and your team. But do participate.

Next, you're going to have to demonstrate what we described previously in this chapter—process and outcome fairness. The latter is the easy one for you, as demonstrated by your success in your former role. And because you are an individual who places a premium on fairness, this is a snap. However, the process fairness component is going to be more difficult. You will have to make a concerted effort to be sure the views of everyone on your team have been heard. Don't cut people off if they ramble a bit, as you have done in your individual contributor role. Provide adequate opportunities for team members to be part of efforts that affect them professionally. For example, if there's a new organizational design that affects staff members, involve them in these changes in whatever way feasible. Process fairness will present enormous dividends to you—and create a more satisfying and productive work environment for your team! In my consulting pratice, I suggested a very successful strategy to a newly promoted manager who was bringing in new staff members. Rather than interviewing the prospective candidates himself or simply involving others in the interviews (which is a great first step toward process fairness, by the way), he asked candidates to help him design the position. Consider this a basic needs assessment method. Provide prospective staff members with the opportunity to help you discern the current needs of your department as well as where the department and organization are headed in the next three years. Share this with those in the human resources area, get their feedback, and give this feedback to your team.

I hope you see from this response, Beth, that you now have to not only act like a leader but think like one as well. If you engage in this strategy, I have high hopes that you'll be as successful a leader as you were an individual contributor.

Louellen Advises...

In my experience, Beth, new managers often worry a little too much about being liked. Consequently, they don't make the hard decisions that come with the role of leader. Your job is to get the results the organization expects. So I would encourage you to think of your goal as gaining the respect of your former peers while competently executing your new duties. Be fair. Be consistent. Be clear about what you expect. Listen to all your staff members and use their input where appropriate. Look for ways of removing barriers to working efficiently. Slowly, you will gain their respect. If there is a sure hit—something like obtaining a much-needed piece of equipment or quickly filling a vacant position—go after it to demonstrate how effective you can be.

In the meantime, let them know who you are as a person. While you have not done much socializing in the past and may not want to do more now, try to incorporate some relationship building into your daily activities. Talk a bit about your family, friends, and interests and, in turn, be curious about your staff members' outside lives. Don't pry too deeply, of course; keep it light and friendly. Once they see your "human" side, I'll bet the tension will ease and your relationships will improve.

You may want to consider an off-site staff retreat to do some team building and have social time together with your group. An outside facilitator might help mediate some of the friction and allow you to relax and even have some fun with your new staff.

Our Final Words of Advice

As we emphasized in the introduction of *Manager's Desktop Consultant*, our aim in writing this book is to help leaders do some of the work that they typically would call on a consultant to perform. Certainly some circumstances are beyond the scope of a leader's time, energy, or skills. We hope we have provided you with some core skills that will help you solve everyday people problems. Kudos to you in advance for attempting to address these often challenging situations. You are now more prepared for the job of leading.

Throughout this book we have integrated not only our own experiences in the leadership and consulting world but also those of many highly regarded experts in the field of leadership and organization development. We have attempted to bring to you, in an abbreviated way, the highlights of some of the finest research and thinking in these areas. Figure 16, a checklist located at the end of this chapter, provides an overview of many suggested key action strategies and should help you synthesize the information in this book. Use it as a list of "to dos" that will create a foundation for your management success.

USING HELPFUL RESOURCES

Our clients often ask us which professional journals they should read either to develop a better grounding in the field of management or to enhance their already highly skilled management repertoire. This is obviously a very difficult question to answer because it depends on your experiences and interests—present and future. But because the question is such a meaningful one, we've developed an abbreviated list of resources. Table 6 contains some of the selected journals and our perspectives on their relationship to the world of management.

As you review many of the articles in these journals, you'll see that there is a tremendous focus on correcting bad situations—whether it be poor organizational performance, inappropriate strategies, inadequate leadership development, or mediocre performance management practices, just to name a few. While this book certainly has focused as well on correcting these types of perennial problems, we hope we have also provided some positive proactive approaches. The power of rewards is one that we would like to mention in our concluding comments.

We have discovered through our clients that a good dose of the appropriate reward can mitigate or at least reduce the intensity of some

TABLE 6. Louellen and Mitch's Top Picks of Professional Journals

Title	Our Perspectives
Harvard Business Review	A must-read for the latest theories and research on leadership and management practices. This journal is particularly adept at focusing on strategy and organizational behavior. Don't be fooled into thinking that it's just for corporate types. It does a good job of addressing the needs of the nonprofit sector as well.
Fortune	Geared to the for-profit world, this magazine has tidbits of organizational information, from soup to nuts.
Leader to Leader	It's the only journal of its kind that focuses on leaders speaking to leaders on timely topics in leadership development.
The Wall Street Journal	While technically not a journal, this newspaper addresses key issues facing the business world.
Consulting to Management	This journal is designed for a consulting audience but often has articles that are written in laypersons' terms. There are useful tips throughout.
Fast Company	This quick read includes many examples of innovative approaches to leadership in all types of organizations.

of the organizational problems mentioned in this book. These rewards are most effective when used *before* concerns turn into significant problems. We suggest that you review the reward structure in your own unit.

And don't think of rewards as only compensation, although that certainly is a viable form. The research on monetary rewards indicates that compensation is just a temporary motivator. It's more important to discern the type of reward that is most meaningful to someone. To help you do this, we suggest two resources: *1001 Ways to Energize Employees* (1997) and *1001 Ways to Reward Employees* (1994), both written by Bob Nelson. You may already be using some of his suggestions, but others may cause you to reflect critically on innovative strategies for increased momentum in your organization.

You may also wish to review the sources we have listed in the References section at the end of the book. These will provide you with ideas we have not explored here.

REFLECTING ON MANAGEMENT AND LEADERSHIP

Finally, we want to leave you with some concluding words of advice— our reflections on management and leadership.

Louellen Advises...

Over the years, I've developed some themes, which I've integrated into my seminars and consultations, to help managers execute their roles more effectively. I offer them to you here as general guidelines to keep in the back of your mind as you continue to develop your management capability.

TAKE CHARGE

Too often I see reluctant managers who seem to fear assuming full responsibility for the work units they are leading. Fear of making the wrong decisions or alienating other people is often the culprit. When you sign up for a management position, accountability for outcomes is yours—no one else's. Problems are yours to solve, and it is important that you not shirk your duty. Instead, step up to the plate and develop some degree of comfort with the pressure you have assumed. Remember that you don't have to go it alone. By using the strategies of engagement and involvement, you can keep your team of staff and colleagues by your side as long as you choose to build those relationships. Don't be a reluctant leader.

MAKE THINGS HAPPEN

Look for opportunities to put your signature on your work. Ask yourself, "When I move on from my current role and look back on what I've left behind, for what will I be known?" You don't want the answer to be, "A lot of loose ends!" Drive activities to implementation without undue delay. Recognize that a sense of accomplishment is a prime motivator for high-achieving staff members. Be known as a leader who gets things done.

GET SMARTER EVERY DAY

I can't emphasize enough the need for managers to continually learn, staying up to date on the technical aspects of their work as well as on leadership development. With rapid change the norm, it is critical to be on top of your game so that you can lead your group in relevant directions and participate in strategy development. Don't be afraid to steal a good idea or two from other leaders you have met or whose books or articles you have read. Just twist your mental kaleidoscope and adapt their ideas to your own context.

LISTEN MORE THAN YOU TALK

As your management career develops, you will find yourself talking more and listening less. You will be called upon to speak, facilitate, and contribute more extensively with each promotion. But don't forget that your most powerful learning tool is the ability to draw information from others and hear their viewpoints and ideas. My experiences have shown that many leaders make a grave mistake when they disconnect from their staff members by no longer giving them a voice. Errors come in the form of bad decisions or lost morale. Don't fall into this trap.

GROW TALENT

One of my favorite authors on leadership—Max DePree (1989), founder of Herman Miller Corporation—said that the art of leadership is in "polishing, liberating, and enabling the gifts" of the people you manage. Set a goal that every person you lead will have an opportunity to find and utilize his or her strengths. Help staff members become better and stronger, even if it means promoting a superstar out of your department or giving an underperformer a risky assignment that offers the chance to develop.

DEVELOP YOUR PERSONAL ADVISORY BOARD

Surround yourself with a cast of people who can offer you counsel and assistance at a moment's notice. Put us at the top of your list, via this book, and then delineate the names of people who might fit these roles: mentor, technical consultant, emotional supporter, organizational "politics" adviser, network developer, information provider (on a given subject area). Make up some of your own categories and expand your resources.

PUT YOUR OWN OXYGEN MASK ON FIRST

No one benefits from daily exposure to a burned-out leader. You must take care of yourself in order to have the energy, concentration, and positive attitude necessary to be an inspiration to others. Self-care includes paying attention to your diet, exercise, health, stress management, and psychological well-being. Remember that you serve as a role model for others, and they deserve your best.

Mitch Advises...

Among the hundreds of leaders I have coached through 360-degree feedback, three areas of concern typically bubble to the top in terms of what staff members want their leaders to do more effectively:

149

- Manage their performance more successfully
- Link long-term strategy and day-to-day operations
- Engage in their career development with greater intensity

I'd like to tackle each of these separately.

MANAGE PERFORMANCE SUCCESSFULLY

In my consulting work, I have often been amazed to find out that many poor performers are actually crying out for good performance management. For example, when I am called in to help a leader work with a "poor performer," I often discover that the manager has not communicated the critical expectations of the task at hand in behaviorally specific and concrete terms.

My advice here is to stop, look, and listen. Make sure that you have explained clearly what it is you are asking someone to do. Certainly, lack of skill in setting expectations is not the root of all performance management problems. In my estimation, though, it's at the top of the list of reasons for distress calls. In addition, don't overlook the fact that performance management also has to do with how you help your star performers, as we have noted in this book. They need good performance management, too.

LINK STRATEGY AND OPERATIONS

I have also discovered that some managers have what I call an "absolute" personality. They are either gifted at focusing on day-to-day operations or, at the opposite extreme, talented at long-term strategy. Effective leaders find ways to marry the two—certainly not in every accountability they have but rather within selected domains. So if you're one of these absolute leaders with a gift at either end of the continuum, find one responsibility that ties the strategic and operational ends together. For example, let's say you are an assistant superintendent of a school district in charge of district-wide instruction. One of your many accountabilities may be to narrow the learning gap among various groups of students. And let's also pretend that you are an operational leader who manages on a yearly rather than a long-term basis. An integrated approach might be to work with the principals at all of the schools in a long-term perspective by giving *them* shorter-term accountabilities for narrowing this gap with their teachers. Essentially, what the leader does is to associate day-to-day operations with the long-term strategic vision of the organization—the mark of a truly successful leader!

ENGAGE IN STAFF MEMBERS' CAREER DEVELOPMENT

Staff members also mention the manager who ignores the career-related concerns of his or her staff. Why would leaders do this? Many are focused on the task at hand—whether it be managing the customer service area, leading a strategic initiative, or reducing patient wait times for physicians—and their myriad other responsibilities. Yet career development emerges as a prime issue in 360-degree feedback from thousands of respondents.

My suggestion is that you, as the leader, become aware that many staff members are concerned about career development. Then talk with them about it. You don't have to provide a plan of action. Sometimes, just by talking, staff members develop their own insights for action. At other times, you simply may not have the skills to do this. In that case, I see two primary avenues. One is to find an expert and refer staff members to this professional. Many organizations employ a human resources professional who is available to tackle such issues. Another is to follow the advice Louellen noted earlier in this chapter: "Get smarter every day." Leaders should read, read, read . . . and not just material specifically related to their particular field. Do a Google search for an article or book about coaching others on career development. Talk with a colleague who seems to have a special knack for this. Whatever you do, make yourself smarter by creating greater opportunities to dialogue with your staff on this top issue of concern to so many.

Finally, be true to yourself. If there are some areas in this book that are just way beyond your comfort level or expertise, that's fine. We aren't saying you should gravitate to all areas. Remember, this book is about two things—doing some things better without a consultant and being more productive by engaging a consultant in more effective ways. We hope *Manager's Desktop Consultant* has provided you with both.

In closing, we want to say that capturing these parting thoughts in a summary format was a rich experience for us because it reaffirmed our beliefs and practices. We have striven to present perplexing, challenging circumstances in workable chunks. While the road to management effectiveness may be bumpy at times, with dauntingly sharp curves, we hope that we have made your journey a bit smoother and more successful.

FIGURE 16. Management and Leadership Checklist

Management

☐ I have a departmental plan that includes goals, objectives, strategies, and action plans.

☐ The plan is driven by the corporate mission and values.

☐ I use effective decision-making skills to choose strategic directions, involving others as much as I can.

☐ The plan is flexible, changing as external and internal events dictate.

☐ My department is organized in a way that maximizes the ability of staff to achieve the organization's goals and objectives.

☐ I optimize the use of teams as an organizing unit.

☐ My department coordinates well with other departments.

☐ I delegate tasks effectively.

☐ I and others organize our workloads effectively.

☐ Job/role descriptions have been written for each position that appears on the organizational chart. They indicate key tasks to be performed, percentages of time, and competencies needed.

☐ A recruiting process is in place that creates an outstanding applicant pool.

☐ A screening process is in place to narrow the applicant pool to those candidates who are most appropriate to the open position.

☐ A selection process is in place that identifies the best candidates.

☐ An orientation process is in place that meets new staff members' information and social needs.

☐ I have developed an effective on-the-job training and orientation program in my department.

☐ Job standards have been established and are communicated before staff members begin a new job.

☐ I give ongoing performance feedback to my staff.

☐ I conduct formal performance reviews as corporate policy requires.

FIGURE 16 *cont'd*

☐ Developmental plans are in place for each staff member in my department.

☐ A compensation plan is in place that is competitive and rewards good performance.

☐ All staffing procedures are conducted in a legal manner in my department.

☐ Quality control indicators (service and product) have been established for each department/division in the company.

☐ I have worked with staff members on established control points for each activity they perform so they can monitor quality for themselves.

☐ My department has an effective method for collecting information about quality.

☐ Quality problems are corrected efficiently and effectively in my department.

☐ If some elements of the strategic plan are not being implemented or are unworkable, I initiate a course correction.

Leadership

☐ My department is open to change, responding to new developments effectively.

☐ I have educated myself on future trends and encourage staff members to do the same.

☐ I encourage staff members to look for new ways of doing things.

☐ I encourage risk taking within appropriate boundaries.

☐ I have fine-tuned my ability to communicate new ideas effectively.

☐ I strive to create a learning environment in my department, so that learning is highly valued and experimentation is encouraged and rewarded.

☐ I have studied the political dynamics of the organization.

FIGURE 16 cont'd

☐ I understand what types of influence strategies are most valued in the organization.

☐ I am skilled in building coalitions with others in order to get things done.

☐ I have a good working relationship with my own manager.

☐ I have good working relationships with other managers.

☐ I understand my own bases of influence.

☐ I strive to empower the staff in our department.

☐ I can motivate others to see the value of an idea, procedure, or change.

☐ I understand the motivational drives of each of my staff members.

☐ I use an abundant amount of praise and recognition with individuals and the team.

☐ When staff members encounter obstacles to job performance, I coach them and try to let them find their own solutions so as to maintain their self-esteem.

☐ I manage conflict effectively; reoccurring problems are infrequent.

☐ Communication flows readily throughout the organization and my department, so staff members get the information they need to do their jobs adequately and to know the purpose of their actions.

☐ I keep the corporate vision alive by talking about it, reinforcing the values.

☐ I and other managers create a team environment by shifting the vision from "ours" to "yours."

☐ I am a strong role model of organizational values.

☐ I have developed a management style that empowers and develops staff members who work with me.

☐ I manage my own stress effectively.

☐ I strive to keep myself motivated so I can, in turn, motivate others.

References

Brockner, J. 2006. Why it's so hard to be fair. *Harvard Business Review* 84, 3 (March): 122–129.

Buckingham, M., and C. Coffman. 1999. *First, break all the rules: What the world's best managers do differently.* New York: Simon and Schuster.

DePree, M. 1989. *Leadership is an art.* New York: Dell.

Essex, L., and M. Kusy. 1999. *Fast forward leadership: How to exchange outmoded leadership practices for forward-looking leadership today.* London: Financial Times Prentice Hall.

Fournies, F. 1987. *Coaching for improved work performance.* Blue Ridge Summit, PA: Liberty House.

Huselid, M. A. 1995. The impact of human resource management practices on turnover, productivity, and corporate financial performance. *Academy of Management Journal* 38, 3:647.

Jacobs, R. W. 1994. *Real time strategic change: How to involve an entire organization in fast and far-reaching change.* San Francisco: Berrett-Koehler.

Jones, A. 1999. *Team-building activities for every group.* Richland, WA: Rec Room.

Kotter, J. P. 1995. Leading change: Why transformations fail. *Harvard Business Review* 73, 2:59.

Kusy, M., and L. Essex. 2005. *Breaking the code of silence: Prominent leaders reveal how they rebounded from seven critical mistakes.* Lapham, MD: Taylor Trade.

Kusy, M., and R. McBain. 2000. Putting real value into strategic planning: Moving beyond never-never land. *Organization Development Practitioner* 32, 2:18–24.

Larson, C. E., and F. M. J. LaFasto. 1989. *Teamwork: What must go right/What can go wrong.* Newbury Park, CA: Sage.

McLagan, P. 2003. The change-capable organization. *T & D* 57, 1 (January): 50–57.

Meyerson, D. E. 2001. Radical change, the quiet way. *Harvard Business Review* 79, 10 (October): 34–42.

Nelson, B. 1994. *1001 ways to reward employees.* New York: Workman.

———. 1997. *1001 ways to energize employees.* New York: Workman.

Nilson, C. 1993. *Team games for trainers.* New York: McGraw-Hill.

Index